The Organix

Baby & Toddler Cookbook

EBURY PRESS

1 3 5 7 9 10 8 6 4 2

Published in 2019 by Ebury Press an imprint of
Ebury Publishing,
20 Vauxhall Bridge Road,
London SW1V 2SA

Ebury Press is part of the Penguin Random House
group of companies whose addresses can be
found at global.penguinrandomhouse.com

Text © Organix Brands Limited 2019
Photography © Haarala Hamilton 2019

Organix has asserted its right to be identified as
the author of this Work in accordance with the
Copyright, Designs and Patents Act 1988

First published by Ebury Press in 2019

www.penguin.co.uk

A CIP catalogue record for this book is available
from the British Library

Design: Louise Evans
Photography: Haarala Hamilton
Food stylist: Kitty Coles
Prop stylist: Faye Wears
Editor: Samantha Crisp

ISBN 9781529103939

The information in this book has been compiled
by way of general guidance in relation to the
specific subjects addressed, but it is not a
substitute and not to be relied on for medical,
healthcare, pharmaceutical or other professional
advice on specific circumstances and in specific
locations. Please consult your GP before changing
your baby's diet. Children should be supervised
while eating, and food sizes and portions should
be adapted to suit individual needs. So far as the
author is aware the information given is correct
and up to date as at December 2018. Practice,
laws and regulations all change, and the reader
should obtain up-to-date professional advice on
any such issue. The author and the publishers
disclaim, as far as the law allows, any liability
arising directly or indirectly from the use, or
misuse, of the information contained in this book.

Printed and bound in China by Toppan Leefung

Penguin Random House is committed to a
sustainable future for our business, our readers
and our planet. This book is made from Forest
Stewardship Council® certified paper.

Hello, we're Organix!

You might recognise us from the baby and toddler food aisle at your local supermarket. As one of the first organic food companies in the UK, we've been cooking up scrummy, nutritious baby and toddler meals and snacks since 1992. All with the reassurance of our No Junk Promise – our pledge to never add anything unnecessary and to only use recognisable ingredients to make good, honest, delicious food.

We really care about good food, just like all you parents out there. That's why we decided a little while back to go one step further, and share some of our favourite recipes to help inspire you in the kitchen – and your little ones too. We know how tough and time-consuming it can be when you're a parent, so hopefully the delicious meals and snacks you'll find in these pages will help make things easier in some small way.

A HEALTHY STARTER

It may seem like common sense to us today, but making sure children ate a varied diet, full of texture and taste from real fruit and veg, was a much less talked-about idea back in 1992, when healthy-eating campaigner Lizzie Vann founded Organix.

After searching in vain for healthy, organic baby and toddler food, she decided to make her own, and Organix was born. It wasn't just a business, but a passion, with a clear vision for the future: creating a world where healthy, nutritious food was a real choice for everyone.

From humble beginnings in her kitchen in Christchurch, Dorset, to the fully-fledged company Organix has become today, we're still doing everything we can to put your little ones' health first.

We create the best-quality food we can with sustainable, organic ingredients. We reject all artificial colours, preservatives, chemicals and pesticides. And we set standards in the food industry.

We actively drive change through our continued campaigns aimed at policy makers, food manufacturers, retailers and consumers, encouraging them to remove unnecessary artificial colours, flavours and preservatives.

And of course, we help parents like you make great food choices. Not just with our tasty finger foods and snacks, but with the scrummy, good-for-little-tummies food you'll soon be preparing with the help of this, our cookbook.

The Organix team on our 25th birthday

OVER 70 SIMPLE RECIPES TO FUEL THEIR WONDER

Written to help busy parents fuel their little ones' wonder with tasty, nutritious food, every recipe in this book has been tried and tested by our own teeny-tiny food critics. From the perfect porridge for baby's breakfast, to a tasty shepherd's pie for the whole family's tea – they all get the little thumbs-up. Better still, they're perfectly portioned, and gentle on growing tummies, too.

As you flick through the following chapters, you'll notice that we've organised our recipes into four age groups: 6+ months, 7+ months, 10+ months and 12+ months. By following these age groups, you can be sure you're always cooking the right food for your child's developmental stage. Starting with easy-to-eat, not-too-sweet, fruit and vegetable purées for babies in the weaning stage at six months.

Once your little ones have learnt to chew and swallow, grown their first baby teeth, and started getting used to different tastes and textures, you can move on to our more grown-up, solid food recipes – including Simple Oaty Waffles, family friendly Pasta and Sauce with Seasonal Veggies, and Spinach and Mushroom Pancakes. They are all designed to have lots of different textures and tastes, to help your budding foodie fall in love with yummy fruit and veg.

'You'll always have something healthy and tasty, ready to go in minutes'

KEEPING THINGS NICE (AND SIMPLE)

Here at Organix, we understand that, as a parent, you've already got your hands full. So instead of making you search out dozens of exotic ingredients, we've kept our recipes nice and simple. The items you'll need to make them are likely to be hiding in your kitchen cupboards, or can easily be found at your local supermarket.

When it comes to fresh fruit and veg, we'd always recommend that you choose organic. But it goes without saying that any fresh produce is better than none at all! And remember, if you can't get hold of fresh fruit and veg, frozen or canned versions are a great option. Often picked and preserved at their freshest, they're still nutritious.

On the topic of frozen food, when you're rushing around after a little one, batch cooking and freezing can become your secret weapon. With this in mind, we've included a few recipes that we love to make in bulk, and freeze in portions. So you'll always have something healthy and tasty, ready to go in minutes.

Last but by no means least, if your little ones have any dietary requirements, such as a gluten or dairy intolerance, or if you're feeding them a vegan or vegetarian diet, you'll find the recipes that are suitable for them are clearly labelled. We've also included substitution ideas, to help you adapt our recipes to suit your little ones.

We hope that you and your family enjoy these recipes as much as we do. With love from all of us at Organix.

LET'S GET COOKING!

A guide to our recipe symbols

Throughout this book we have included symbols to show the recipes that accommodate different dietary requirements and to highlight recipes that are great for freezing in batches.

We've also included notes in the ingredients lists to show where some recipes can be easily adapted for your little ones.

(v) Vegan   (V) Vegetarian

(gf) Gluten free   (df) Dairy free

❄ Can be frozen for up to one month

NOTE: All eggs used are free-range and medium size, unless otherwise stated.

All portion sizes are suggested for the indicated age group of the recipe, unless otherwise stated.

Consult your GP before feeding young children nuts. Mixed spices and other ingredients may contain traces of nuts.

Breakfast

All our first purées are here to help at the very start of your little one's weaning journey. As you and your baby progress, try adding some herbs or spices to start gently introducing lots of exciting tastes and flavours.

MANGO PURÉE

PREP: under 10 minutes

MAKES: lots of portions – ideal for freezing in ice-cube trays for weaning

1 ripe mango, peeled, stoned and roughly chopped
a little water (if needed)

1. In a bowl, blend the mango to a smooth purée, adding some water if required (just enough to get the right consistency). A hand blender will give the smoothest texture, but a food processor or blender can also be used.

2. For an even smoother texture, push the purée through a fine sieve.

PEAR PURÉE

PREP: under 10 minutes

COOK: 20–30 minutes

MAKES: lots of portions – ideal for freezing in ice-cube trays for weaning

1-2 pears, peeled, cored and quartered
a little water (if needed)

1. Steam the pears until soft, about 20 minutes, either using a steamer or by placing in a colander over a pan of simmering water and covering (you could boil the pear instead, if you prefer).

2. In a bowl, blend the pear to a smooth purée, adding some water if required (just enough to get the right consistency). A hand blender will give the smoothest texture, but a food processor or blender can also be used.

3. For an even smoother texture, push the purée through a fine sieve.

BREAKFAST

BANANA PURÉE

PREP: 10 minutes

MAKES: lots of portions – ideal for freezing in ice-cube trays for weaning

1 ripe banana, peeled and chopped
a little water (if needed)

1. In a bowl, blend the banana to a smooth purée. This can be done with a fork, but a hand blender will give the smoothest texture (a food processor or blender can also be used).

2. For an even smoother texture, push the purée through a fine sieve.

VEGGIE SMOOTHIE

PREP: 10 minutes

MAKES: 1 large or 2 small smoothies

1 small apple
(about 120g/4½oz)
70g (3oz) frozen
cauliflower florets
25g (1oz) frozen peas
20g (¾oz) baby spinach
leaves
175ml (6fl oz/¾cup) water

This green smoothie is loaded with vegetables. The secret ingredient is frozen cauliflower to make it extra smooth and silky. For little ones over 12 months, add 1-2 teaspoons of seeds such as pumpkin, sunflower or flaxseed for added goodness.

1. Cut the apple into quarters and remove the core and pips.

2. Put the apple into a blender with all the remaining ingredients and whizz until smooth.

BANANA FIG PORRIDGE

PREP: 10 minutes

COOK: under 10 minutes

MAKES: 1–2 servings

1 tbsp oats (gluten free
   if required)
3 tbsp water
½ dried fig, finely chopped
1 small ripe banana,
   peeled and mashed

This is a favourite early recipe for lots of little ones starting out on their weaning journey. For older babies, you could add a few slices of banana for added texture.

1. Put the oats and the water into a small pan and bring to the boil. Reduce the heat, cover and simmer for about 5 minutes, stirring occasionally to prevent sticking.

2. Remove the porridge from the heat and stir in the chopped fig, then set aside to cool slightly.

3. Add the mashed banana and mix with a fork until well combined. Blend to a smooth texture for a first weaning recipe or serve as a rough mash for older babies.

BANANA RAISIN PORRIDGE

PREP: 10 minutes

COOK: under 10 minutes

MAKES: 2–3 servings

3 tbsp oats (gluten free
   if required)
150ml (5fl oz/⅔ cup) water
1 small ripe banana, peeled
   and mashed
2 tsp raisins

A simple and tasty breakfast for little ones to start the day with. For older babies, you could add a few slices of banana for added texture.

1. Put all the ingredients into a small pan and bring to the boil.

2. Reduce the heat, cover and simmer gently for about 5 minutes, stirring occasionally to stop it from sticking to the bottom of the pan.

3. Purée by pushing through a sieve or by whizzing with a hand blender. Add more water if a thinner consistency is preferred.

PORRIDGE with FRUITY COMPOTE

PREP: 10 minutes

COOK: 20-30 minutes

MAKES: 6-8 servings

FOR THE COMPOTE:
1 medium apple, peeled,
   cored and diced
1 pear, peeled, cored
   and diced
3 large dates, cut into
   raisin-sized pieces
large handful of mixed
   dried fruit
grated zest and juice of
   1 orange
pinch of ground cinnamon
1 tsp vanilla extract
pinch of grated nutmeg
2 cloves

FOR THE PORRIDGE:
55g (2oz/¼ cup) oats
   (gluten free if required)
250ml (8fl oz/1 cup)
   full-fat milk
½ tsp vanilla extract

A thoroughly fruity breakfast that the whole family can enjoy. Make sure you purée or mash the porridge and compote to the right texture for your little one. For little ones over 6 months this recipe can be served with a dollop of full-fat yoghurt for a tasty change.

1. Put all the compote ingredients into a pan and cook over a low-medium heat until the fruits are tender, about 20 minutes.

2. Remove the orange peel and cloves.

3. For the porridge, combine the oats, milk and vanilla in a pan and stir over a medium heat until smooth and thick, about 10 minutes.

4. Purée or mash the compote to the right texture for your little one, then serve the porridge with the warm fruity compote spooned on top.

TOP TIP: stick the cloves into a piece of orange peel to prevent them from getting lost in the mixture.

ALMOND & CINNAMON PORRIDGE

7+ months

 (df)

PREP: 10 minutes

COOK: about 10 minutes

MAKES: 1 adult and 1 baby portion

50g (2oz/¼ cup) oats (gluten free if required)
50g (2oz/½ cup) ground almonds (see page 7)
1 tsp ground cinnamon
250ml (8fl oz/1 cup) water or milk of your choice

OPTIONAL TOPPINGS:
drizzle of maple syrup
sprinkle of pumpkin seeds (12+ months)
sprinkle of sunflower seeds (12+ months)
large handful of fresh strawberries (or whatever fruit is in season), chopped into bite-sized pieces
dollop of Greek yoghurt

Porridge is a wonderful real-food breakfast and our almond option is lovely and creamy. Good-quality whole oats are super-sustaining and will keep Goldilocks and your little 'bear' full up until lunch. The almonds provide protein and healthy fat, while also giving a natural creaminess, which means you can make the porridge with water instead of milk for a dairy-free version.

1. Tip the oats and ground almonds into a pan.

2. Stir in the cinnamon and water (or milk) and cook over a medium-low heat, stirring regularly, for about 10 minutes until nice and thick.

3. Pour the cooked porridge into bowls then add any or all of the optional toppings. Setting the toppings out on the breakfast table means that little ones can help themselves and will encourage them to get creative - a couple of strawberries and a few seeds can make a great porridge face or an abstract piece of art!

TOP TIP: if you have a set of measuring cups ¼ cup holds exactly 50g oats - it's much easier to use this each morning rather than getting out the scales every day. If you don't have a proper ¼ measuring cup, anything will do that holds the right amount.

EASY PANCAKES

10+ months

PREP: 5 minutes

COOK: 20-30 minutes

MAKES: about 10 pancakes

2 eggs
1 ripe banana, peeled
coconut oil or vegetable oil,
   for frying

TO SERVE:
fresh strawberries (or other
   seasonal fruit if you prefer)
natural or Greek yoghurt
   (use a dairy-free yoghurt
   such as coconut yoghurt
   if you prefer)

These simple pancakes could not be easier or tastier! Serve with seasonal ripe strawberries and yoghurt for a breakfast treat or dessert.

1. Blend the eggs and banana in a blender or food processor until smooth.

2. Heat a drop of oil in a small frying pan (skillet) over a medium heat.

3. Add a ladle of batter to form a small pancake about 6cm (2½in) across. Allow it to cook for 2–3 minutes; when bubbles form on the top flip it over and cook the other side. Repeat until you have used up all the batter. You can cook a few at a time in a larger pan if you prefer and keep the cooked pancakes warm in a low oven while you cook the rest.

BLUEBERRY OATMEAL BAKE

PREP: 10 minutes

COOK: 30 minutes

MAKES: 6–8 servings

2 ripe bananas (riper
   bananas are sweeter)

4 tbsp maple syrup

4 tbsp coconut oil, vegetable
   oil or butter

2 eggs

1 tsp vanilla extract

250ml (8fl oz/1 cup) milk of
   your choice (full-fat cow's
   milk, coconut, almond etc.)

200g (7oz/1 cup) oats
   (gluten free if required)

small handful of raisins (or
   dried cranberries if you
   prefer)

150g (5oz) fresh or frozen
   blueberries (defrosted if
   frozen)

This simple, tasty recipe makes the most of seasonal blueberries but, if blueberries are out of season, you can swap them for cranberries or blackberries. Serve warm in a bowl for breakfast or as a dessert, perhaps with a little natural yoghurt. Or allow to cool then slice into bars.

1. Preheat the oven to 180°C/160°C fan/350°F/gas mark 4.

2. Put the bananas, maple syrup, oil or butter, eggs, vanilla and milk into a blender and blitz until completely smooth (if you don't have a blender, mash the bananas to a purée then whisk with all other wet ingredients).

3. Put the oats into a baking dish about 30 x 20cm (12 x 8in). Pour the wet mixture over and stir to mix completely, then stir through the raisins and blueberries.

4. Bake for about 30 minutes, until golden and set.

VARIATION: It's good to introduce children to tart and bitter flavours to educate their palate. However, if your little one finds this recipe too tart you can add some natural sweetness with an orange – orange and cranberry really complement each other. Prepare the wet ingredients as above and set aside. Simmer the raisins and 150g cranberries with the zest and juice of 1 orange in a pan over a medium-low heat for 10 minutes, or until the cranberries pop. Allow it to cool slightly, then blitz in a blender until thick and smooth. Combine the oats and wet mixture in a baking dish as above, then simply swirl the puréed cranberries through the creamy oat mixture and bake until set. You can create a beautiful marble pattern with the two colours. It takes a little longer but will be sweeter for little taste buds.

FRUITY BANANA BREAD

10+ months

PREP: 10–15 minutes

COOK: 40–45 minutes

MAKES: 10 slices

170g (6oz) ripe banana, peeled
70ml (2½fl oz) vegetable oil
2 eggs
120ml (4fl oz/½ cup) water
1 tsp vanilla extract
250g (9oz/2 cups) self-raising flour (gluten free if required)
2 tsp baking powder
1 tsp bicarbonate of soda (baking soda)
½ tsp ground cinnamon
80g (3oz) raisins

A simple, tasty recipe that is great for breakfast or at snack times. Good on its own but to make it extra tasty, why not spread on a little butter?

1. Preheat the oven to 200°C/180°C fan/400°F/gas mark 6 and grease and line a 450g (1lb) loaf tin.

2. Mash the banana, place it in a large bowl with the oil, eggs, water and vanilla and beat until creamy.

3. Sift in the flour, baking powder, bicarbonate of soda and cinnamon and stir in the raisins.

4. Spoon into the prepared tin and level the surface. Bake for 40–45 minutes, or until a knife comes out clean when inserted in the middle.

5. Turn out on to a wire rack and leave to cool before slicing.

FRENCH TOAST with WINTER COMPOTE

(V) (df)

PREP: 10 minutes

COOK: 15–20 minutes

MAKES: 4 servings

FOR THE COMPOTE:
1 clove
4 ripe plums, stoned and cut into bite-sized pieces
½ tsp ground cinnamon
1 tsp vanilla extract
3 tbsp water

FOR THE FRENCH TOAST:
2 eggs
1 tsp vanilla extract
pinch of ground cinnamon
2 large slices of wholemeal bread
sunflower oil, for frying

This makes a tasty winter breakfast but you could use other seasonal fruits for the compote to make this great at any time of the year. Serve with a dollop of the plum compote on the side or some yoghurt and fresh fruit pieces.

1. First make the compote. Stick the clove into the skin of one of the plum pieces so it's easier to retrieve later, then put all the ingredients into a small pan and cook over a low heat until the fruit has softened and cooked down, about 10 minutes. Remove from the heat and remove and discard the clove.

2. While the compote is cooking, beat the eggs in a bowl together with the vanilla and cinnamon.

3. Spread one slice of bread with the plum compote then place the other slice on top to make a sandwich. Carefully dip into the egg mixture to coat both sides (you can cut the sandwich in half if it makes it easier to dip).

4. Heat a little oil in a frying pan (skillet) until hot, then place the sandwich in the hot pan to cook until golden on one side. Flip over to cook the other side, then when golden remove from the pan. Allow to cool a little, then cut into fingers and serve.

KEDGEREE

PREP: 10 minutes

COOK: under 30 minutes

MAKES: 2–3 portions

1 egg
80g (3oz) white rice
2 cardamom pods
1 tbsp unsalted butter
1 small onion, diced
½ tsp mild curry powder
handful of baby spinach
   leaves (about 60g/2½oz)
1 fillet of cooked, line-caught
   white or oily fish (such as
   haddock or mackerel)

A tasty fishy recipe, great for little ones growing up. Why not let them explore the textures with their fingers or try a spoon or fork?

1. Bring a small pan of water to the boil and hard-boil the egg for about 8–10 minutes. Cool under the cold tap; when cool enough to handle peel and chop into about 8 pieces.

2. Meanwhile, cook the rice with the cardamom pods according to the packet instructions, until the rice is tender. Drain and set aside.

3. Melt the butter in a large frying pan (skillet), add the onion and sauté over a low heat for about 5 minutes until the onion is soft and has absorbed the butter. Add the curry powder and continue to sauté for another minute.

4. Add the spinach and allow it to wilt, before adding the rice (remove the cardamom pods first) and stir until the rice is a nice yellow colour.

5. Carefully remove any skin and bones from the cooked fish fillet, then flake with a fork. Add to the rice, give it all a good stir and then serve with the pieces of chopped egg on top. If your little one isn't quite ready for the texture of this recipe, you can blend or mash it down to suit them.

BREAKFAST FRITTATA CUPS

PREP: under 10 minutes

COOK: 20–30 minutes

MAKES: 12 frittata cups

**vegetable oil, for greasing
and frying
4 large open cap mushrooms,
finely chopped
6 large eggs
120ml (4fl oz/½ cup)
full-fat milk (a non-dairy
alternative or even water
will also work if you prefer)
large handful of spinach,
finely chopped
100g (4oz) hard cheese
(such as Cheddar), grated**

A great way to start the day! These are also great for lunchboxes and picnics or as a snack at any time of day. Keep in the fridge for a couple of days or freeze; defrost thoroughly or heat through for 15 minutes in the oven before serving.

1. Preheat the oven to 200°C/180°C fan/400°F/gas mark 6 and lightly grease a 12-hole muffin tin (pan) with oil.

2. Heat a drizzle of oil in a frying pan (skillet) over a medium heat and sauté the mushrooms for a few minutes, then leave to cool slightly.

3. Whisk together the eggs and milk, then stir in the spinach, cooled mushrooms and grated cheese.

4. Pour evenly into the holes of the greased muffin tin and bake for about 20 minutes, or until golden and the egg is cooked through. Allow to cool slightly before serving.

BREAKFAST CORN MUFFINS

PREP: 10–20 minutes

COOK: 25–30 minutes

MAKES: 10 muffins

100ml (3½fl oz/scant ½ cup) olive oil, plus extra for greasing
250ml (8fl oz/1 cup) full-fat milk (or dairy-free alternative of choice)
2 eggs
75g (3oz) grated Parmesan cheese or vegetarian equivalent
100g (4oz) feta cheese, crumbled
2 handfuls of spinach, finely chopped
handful of basil leaves, finely chopped
about 8 cherry tomatoes, chopped
2 spring onions (scallions), finely chopped
200g (7oz/1½ cups) self-raising flour (or gluten free alternative)
150g (5oz) polenta (cornmeal)

The polenta gives a delicious crunchy bite to these savoury muffins, making a refreshing change for breakfast. Serve warm or cold (they can be gently reheated in a warm oven), on their own as a snack, or with some salad and dip for a light lunch.

1. Preheat the oven to 160°C/140°C fan/325°F/gas mark 3 and lightly grease a 12-hole muffin tin (pan) with oil.

2. Whisk together the milk, eggs and oil in a large bowl. Stir in the Parmesan, feta, spinach, basil, tomatoes and spring onions and mix well.

3. Combine the flour and polenta in a separate bowl and then lightly stir into the mixture with a metal spoon.

4. Spoon the mixture into the muffin tin and bake for 20–25 minutes until golden and set.

5. Allow to cool in the tin for about 5 minutes before removing carefully and transferring to a wire rack.

SIMPLE OATY WAFFLES

PREP: 15–30 minutes

COOK: about 10 minutes

MAKES: 4 square waffles

180g (6oz/scant 1 cup) oats
(gluten free if required)
470ml (16fl oz/2 cups) water
1 tbsp maple syrup or honey
(optional)
a little vegetable or coconut
oil, for greasing the waffle
plates

TO SERVE:
non-dairy or Greek yoghurt
fresh seasonal fruit
drizzle of maple syrup or
honey (optional)

EQUIPMENT:
**You'll need a waffle maker
to make these but if you
don't have one you could
cook them on a griddle pan
and simply flip them over
halfway through – although
a waffle maker gives the
best results!**

**These tasty waffles can be whipped up in minutes to impress the family!
Try cutting them up into waffle fingers – perfect for smaller hands.
They look and taste better with just a tablespoon of honey or maple
syrup blended into the mixture, as it helps make the waffle go golden
and a little crispier. You can make these in advance and store in the fridge
for up to 2 days.**

1. Put the oats into a blender and pour over the water. It should only just cover the oats. Add the maple syrup or honey, if using, and blend until smooth.

2. Now allow the mixture to stand for about 10 minutes – it's very important to achieve the right consistency! The oats will absorb the water and swell, so the mixture will become thicker. You want it to be about the consistency of porridge and you should be able to pour it very slowly out of the blender jug on to the waffle plates. If it doesn't 'creep' then it's too thick and if it 'runs' then it's too thin. If too thin try leaving a little longer, and if it becomes too thick you can blend in a tiny drop more water.

3. While the mixture is thickening, brush just a little oil on to the waffle plates and then turn on and allow to heat up, following your waffle maker instructions.

4. Once hot, spoon some mixture on to the plates, avoiding the edges as it will spread out while cooking. Close the lid and cook for about 7 minutes (this may be a bit of trial and error with your own waffle maker). The waffles should be a little crispy on the outside and soft and fluffy on the inside when done.

5. Carefully use a rubber spatula to remove the waffles and keep warm in the oven while you cook the remaining waffles. Serve with yoghurt, seasonal fruit and a drizzle of honey or maple syrup, if liked.

OVERNIGHT OATS

12+ months

(V)

PREP: 10 minutes

MAKES: 1-2 servings

2 dried apricots, chopped
 into bite-sized pieces
50g (2oz/¼ cup) oats
 (gluten free if required)
1 tbsp sunflower seeds
150ml (5fl oz/⅔ cup) milk
 of choice
1 orange
drizzle of maple syrup,
 to serve (optional)

A super-healthy, quick and easy breakfast that all the family will enjoy. Soaking the oats and seeds overnight not only makes this a quick and convenient breakfast, it also makes it far more digestible - great for little ones. This recipe is just one example of overnight oats; you and your family can have fun making your own creations by varying the fruits, seeds and toppings. Serve cold or warm through gently if you prefer.

1. Add to chopped apricots to a bowl with the oats, seeds and milk. Stir to combine.

2. Cover and leave in the fridge overnight.

3. At breakfast, cut the peel and pith off the orange and cut into segments. Arrange these on top of the oaty mixture before serving. Add a drizzle of maple syrup, if you like.

FRUITY EGGY BREAD

12+ months

(V)

PREP: under 10 minutes

COOK: under 10 minutes

MAKES: 1 serving

1 egg
splash of milk
1 slice of wholemeal bread
coconut or vegetable oil,
 for frying
fresh fruit, to serve

A simple and tasty meal that's nice and quick to whip up. Top with fruits - we love berries and banana slices or try with halved cherry tomatoes for a savoury option.

1. Crack the egg into a bowl and whisk with a splash of milk.

2. Cut the bread into fingers, then soak in the egg mixture.

3. Heat a little oil in a frying pan (skillet) over a low-medium heat. Fry the eggy bread for a few minutes on each side until golden brown. Serve with a selection of fruits - those in season tend to taste the best.

RICOTTA PANCAKE WITH SALMON & POACHED EGG

PREP: 10–30 minutes

COOK: 10–15 minutes

MAKES: 2 servings

FOR THE PANCAKES:
250g (9oz) ricotta cheese
125ml (4fl oz/½ cup)
full-fat milk
2 large eggs, separated
100g (4oz/scant 1 cup)
plain flour (gluten free
if required)
1 tsp baking powder
3 tsp chopped chives,
plus extra for sprinkling
coconut or vegetable oil,
for frying

FOR THE TOP:
2 eggs
2 fillets of poached salmon,
cooked and flaked

A tasty meal for growing toddlers as well as the whole family. This is a lovely recipe for when you have that little bit of extra time, making it a great weekend breakfast.

1. Put the ricotta, milk and egg yolks into a medium bowl and mix well to combine. Stir in the flour, baking powder and chives and whisk into a smooth batter. In a separate bowl whisk the egg whites until they become foamy and then fold them into the ricotta mixture.

2. Poach the eggs: bring a pan of water to the boil and then reduce the heat to a gentle simmer. Stir the water to create a small whirlpool and then break the eggs into the water. Cook for 3–4 minutes, then lift out with a slotted spoon on to kitchen paper.

3. Meanwhile, heat the oil in a large frying pan (skillet) and drop in a ladle of batter. Cook the pancakes one at a time, for about 1 minute until golden and then flip them over and cook for another minute. Keep warm in a low oven while you cook the remaining pancakes.

4. Place 2 or 3 pancakes on each plate, top with the flaked salmon, then a poached egg and sprinkle with some chives. Serve warm.

Lunch

COURGETTE PURÉE

PREP: under 10 minutes

COOK: about 20 minutes

MAKES: lots of portions – ideal for freezing in ice-cube trays for weaning

1–2 courgettes (zucchini), thickly sliced
a little water (if needed)

A great first purée to help you get started with weaning. As you and your little one progress, why not add some herbs or spices to start gently introducing lots of exciting tastes and flavours?

1. Steam the courgettes until soft, about 20 minutes, either using a steamer or by placing in a colander over a pan of simmering water and covering (you could boil the courgettes instead, if you prefer).

2. In a bowl, blend the courgettes to a smooth purée, adding some water if required (just enough to get the right consistency). A hand blender will give the smoothest texture, but a food processor or blender can also be used.

3. For an even smoother texture, push the purée through a fine sieve.

BROCCOLI & CARROT PURÉE

PREP: under 10 minutes

COOK: 20–30 minutes

MAKES: lots of portions – ideal for freezing in ice-cube trays for weaning

handful of broccoli florets, halved
1 carrot, peeled and chopped
a little water (if needed)

This is a great combination for when you are at the very start of your little one's weaning journey.

1. Steam the broccoli and carrot together until soft, 20–30 minutes, either using a steamer or by placing in a colander over a pan of simmering water and covering (you could boil the carrots instead, if you prefer).

2. In a bowl, blend to a smooth purée, adding some water if required (just enough to get the right consistency). A hand blender will give the smoothest texture, but a food processor or blender can also be used.

3. For an even smoother texture, push the purée through a fine sieve.

CARROT & KALE PURÉE

PREP: under 10 minutes

COOK: 15–20 minutes

MAKES: lots of portions – ideal for freezing in ice-cube trays for weaning

5 large carrots, peeled and
    thickly sliced
5 large stems of curly kale,
    tough stems removed and
    leaves finely chopped
splash of water (if needed)
herbs or spices of your
    choice (optional)
butter or oil (optional)

A simple seasonal recipe that can be served as a purée for younger babies or as a chunky mash for older babies, although older children and adults may also enjoy the smoother texture you get from blending it, so play around with both. Try adding various herbs, spices and a little butter or oil – it makes a delicious side dish for the rest of the family served with some fish or meat.

1. Steam the carrots for about 15–20 minutes until soft (or boil if you prefer). Add the kale to the steamer for the last 5 minutes so that it wilts but stays bright green.

2. For younger babies, place the vegetables in a blender and blend to a smooth purée. Add a little water if needed to get the desired consistency. For slightly older babies place the drained vegetables in a large bowl and mash together. This textured mash is great for babies starting to explore different textures, so adjust it to suit your little one.

3. This purée is perfect as it is, but you can add herbs or spices if you like. A pinch of turmeric adds a delicate flavour, a little grating of nutmeg can enhance the flavour of the kale, and some fresh coriander can be quite delicious too. You can also add a knob of butter or a splash of olive or hemp oil for some healthy fat.

CHEESE, LEEK & POTATO BAKE

PREP: 10–30 minutes

COOK: 45–60 minutes

MAKES: 3–4 servings

splash of olive oil
½ onion, finely chopped
2 leeks, finely chopped
**2 medium potatoes, peeled
   and thinly sliced**
**100g hard cheese, grated
   (Cheddar works well here)**
**about 150ml (5fl oz/⅔ cup)
   milk**

**A simple tasty meal that can be served with some salad or extra greens
for a satisfying meal.**

1. Preheat the oven to 200°C/180°C fan/400°F/gas mark 6.

2. Heat the olive oil in a frying pan (skillet) and sauté the onion and leeks over a low heat until soft, about 10 minutes.

3. Take a small baking dish (about 20 x 10cm/8 x 4in) and start adding layers, starting with sliced potato, then cheese, then the sautéed leek mixture, and finishing with a layer of cheese. Carefully pour the milk in between the potato slices so it fills the dish and gently press the layers down into the milk.

4. Bake for about 45 minutes, until the cheese is golden and the potato is soft when tested with a knife. Allow to cool before serving. You can mash or purée for younger babies.

CHICKEN WINTER WONDER POT

PREP: 10–30 minutes

COOK: 60+ minutes

MAKES: 2 adult and 2 baby portions

olive oil, for frying
4 chicken thighs (skin on and bone in)
2 onions, finely chopped
2 garlic cloves, crushed
1 tsp ground turmeric
2 tsp ground coriander
2 tsp paprika
2 tsp garam masala
2 sprigs of fresh rosemary, leaves finely chopped
4 sprigs of fresh thyme, leaves finely chopped
1 large parsnip or ¼ swede, scrubbed and diced
4 large carrots, scrubbed and diced
1 leek, chopped
2 x 400g (14oz) cans chopped tomatoes
2 tbsp tomato purée
about 500ml (16fl oz/2 cups) water
large handful of kale, tough stems discarded, leaves shredded

This one-pot wonder is simple, healthy, cheap and easy to make in bulk. Serve with a hunk of good-quality fresh bread for adults, or with brown rice.

1. Seal the chicken thighs for a couple of minutes in a casserole dish over a medium-high heat, with a small drizzle of oil. Once lightly browned remove from the pan and set aside on a plate.

2. Add a drizzle more oil to the pan and sauté the onions for about 5 minutes, until soft. Add the garlic and ground spices and then return the chicken to the pan and stir to coat in the spices.

3. Add the herbs and chopped vegetables (except the kale), then add the canned tomatoes and tomato purée. Pour in enough water so that everything is just submerged.

4. Bring to a gentle boil, then reduce to a low simmer and cook with a lid on for 30 minutes, then without the lid for another 30 minutes, or until the liquid has reduced and become thick.

5. Add the kale leaves to the casserole for the last 5 minutes of cooking to allow them to wilt.

6. Carefully remove the chicken thighs from the casserole with a large slotted spoon and place them on a chopping board. Remove the skin and bones and chop the meat into bite-sized pieces. Return the chopped chicken to the casserole and serve. You can adjust the size of the chicken pieces and veg to suit your little one, or the stew can be mashed or puréed for younger babies.

MINTY PEA & LEEK RISOTTO

7+ months

  (V) (gf)

PREP: under 10 minutes

COOK: 10–30 minutes

MAKES: 3 big portions

1 tbsp olive oil
½ leek (50g), finely chopped
1 garlic clove, finely
   chopped
50g Arborio rice
300ml (10fl oz/1¼ cups)
   water
50g petits pois (defrosted
   if frozen)
sprinkle of dried or fresh mint,
   finely chopped
1 tbsp unsalted butter
1 tbsp cream cheese or
   grated cheese

A fresh and tasty meal for your little one that introduces them to the wonderful combination of pea and mint. Add stir-fried chicken pieces to boost the protein content and to make this into a recipe the whole family will enjoy.

1. Heat the oil in a medium pan, add the leek and garlic and fry until softened, about 5 minutes.

2. Add the rice and fry for about 2 minutes, stirring to coat in the oil.

3. Gradually add the water, a little at a time and stirring continuously. With each addition, wait until the rice has absorbed all the water before adding any more. Add the peas with the last addition of water.

4. Once the rice is soft and has absorbed all the water, add the mint and stir in the butter and cream cheese or grated cheese to give a silky texture.

5. Mash or whizz in a blender to suit your baby's texture requirements – if you need the rice to be runnier just add some milk.

RAINBOW MUFFINS

  ❄

PREP: 10–30 minutes

COOK: 20–30 minutes

MAKES: 10 muffins

225g (8oz/scant 2 cups)
  self-raising flour (gluten
  free if required)
1 small carrot, peeled
  and grated
2 spring onions (scallions),
  finely chopped
½ red (bell) pepper,
  deseeded and finely
  chopped
2 tbsp sweetcorn
100g mature Cheddar
  cheese, grated
175ml (6fl oz/¾ cup) milk
  (or dairy-free alternative)
1 large egg
50ml (2fl oz) olive oil

This is for little ones who love a rainbow! A popular savoury choice for parties, play dates, picnics or just a light lunch or snack. Serve warm or cold; they can be gently reheated in a warm oven.

1. Preheat the oven to 200°C/180°C fan/400°F/gas mark 6 and lightly brush 10 moulds of a 12-hole muffin tin (pan) with oil.

2. Sift the flour into a large bowl and add the carrot, spring onions, red pepper, sweetcorn and grated cheese. Mix well to combine.

3. In a separate bowl, mix together the milk, egg and olive oil. Pour into the bowl of dry ingredients and mix well. Spoon the mixture evenly into the 10 oiled muffin tin holes.

4. Bake for about 20 minutes, until cooked through and golden brown.

5. Cool on a wire rack then pack in an airtight box.

SPEEDY SAVOURY FLAPJACKS

PREP: 10-30 minutes

COOK: 25-30 minutes

MAKES: about 18 flapjacks

200g (7oz) carrots, peeled
300g (10oz/1½ cups) oats
   (gluten free if required)
200g (7oz) mature Cheddar
   cheese, grated
50g (2oz) sunflower seeds,
   finely chopped (optional)
50g (2oz) walnuts, cashews
   or other nuts, finely
   chopped (see page 7;
   optional)
4 tsp dried or finely chopped
   fresh herbs such as
   rosemary or thyme
200g (7oz) butter (or use
   170ml/6fl oz/¾ cup
   olive oil)

All the family will love these savoury cheesy flapjacks. Serve with some fresh apple or pear slices. For a slightly less rich flapjack you can either use olive oil or reduce the butter to 100g (4oz) and add one beaten egg instead. The egg also makes a slightly softer flapjack, which can be good for younger babies. Why not try both and see which you prefer?

1. Preheat the oven to 180°C/160°C fan/350°F/gas mark 4 and lightly grease a 25 x 20cm flapjack tin.

2. Wash and top and tail the carrots, then grate into a large bowl (for speedy flapjacks, use a food processor with the grating attachment). Add the oats and grated Cheddar to the bowl.

3. Add the seeds and nuts, if using, to the bowl. You can crush them with a pestle and mortar or food processor first if they're for younger babies. Add the herbs and stir well.

4. Melt the butter in a pan over a very low heat for a couple of minutes, until just liquid – don't let it burn! Pour the butter over the oat mixture and stir until completely coated. If using oil instead, simply mix in well.

5. Tip into the prepared tin and press down, then bake in the oven for 25 minutes, or until golden.

6. Cut the flapjack into squares while still warm but leave to cool in the tin for 15 minutes. Carefully remove using a palette knife and transfer to a wire rack, until you can resist them no longer!

CARROT & CHEESE BAKES

  (V) (gf) ❄

PREP: 10-30 minutes

COOK: 10-15 minutes

MAKES: 15-20 bakes

2 medium carrots, peeled
  and finely grated
70g (3oz) Cheddar cheese,
  finely grated
2 eggs, beaten
6 level tbsp flour of your
  choice (gluten free options
  such as buckwheat, rice or
  oat all work well)

These savoury bakes can be shaped however you like, even into little carrots – great for getting little ones excited about nibbling on them. If you make the mixture into carrot shapes, try serving on a plate with a little lettuce or some parsley leaves at the top of each carrot – to look like green carrot tops! You could even try pressing the mixture out and cutting with cookie cutters, perhaps a rabbit cutter. They're great for older babies as they have a wonderful soft chewy texture – perfect for weaning.

1. Preheat your oven to 200°C/180°C fan/400°F/gas mark 6 and line a baking tray with baking parchment.

2. Mix all the ingredients together in a large bowl and use clean, damp hands to form a dough.

3. Take a tablespoon of the mixture and form into a ball, then place on the lined tray and press flat, creating a round biscuit shape no more than 5mm (¼in) thick. You can also create long finger shapes, and even triangle 'carrot' biscuits – whatever you fancy.

4. Bake for 10-15 minutes until golden and slightly crisp at the edges. Allow to cool slightly, then transfer to a wire rack to cool completely.

TOP TIP: these are best eaten on the day but can be kept in the fridge for a couple of days in an airtight container.

BROCCOLI & CHEESE SCONE BITES

10+ months

PREP: 10-30 minutes

COOK: about 35 minutes

MAKES: 25 scones

oil, for greasing
½ medium head of broccoli,
    cut into small florets (stem
    discarded)
350g (12oz) self-raising flour
    (or use gluten free flour)
150g (5oz) cold unsalted
    butter, diced
bunch of fresh basil or
    other herbs, leaves finely
    chopped
100g (4oz) grated Cheddar
    cheese
50g (2oz/½ cup) grated
    Parmesan cheese or
    vegetarian equivalent
60ml (2fl oz/¼ cup) milk

These delicious little bites are so easy to make and are a fantastic way of getting some healthy broccoli into your little one. You could also try switching the broccoli for other seasonal veggies, such as grated courgette or butternut squash. Why not also try different herbs to match? Serve warm or cold with a little unsalted butter or a slice of cheese, or just as they are. They are also delicious served instead of bread with a bowl of warming soup.

1. Preheat the oven to 200°C/180°C fan/400°F/gas mark 6 and lightly grease a baking sheet.

2. Steam or boil the broccoli for 5-6 minutes until just soft, but still bright green. Drain and rinse under cold water, then finely chop.

3. Tip the flour into a bowl, add the cold butter and rub into the flour with your fingertips until you have a crumbly texture (or you can use the pulse setting on a food processor instead). Add the basil, both cheeses and the chopped broccoli to the mixture and combine well with your fingers, or the pulse setting on your food processor, being careful not to over-mix.

4. Add the milk, a little at a time, to bring the mixture into a soft dough. Add extra flour or milk if needed – the dough should be light and soft and not too sticky. Knead together lightly.

5. Place the dough on the greased baking sheet and gently press and shape into a square about 3cm (1in) deep. Cut into 25 little bite-sized squares and then separate to give them a little space on the tray

6. Bake for 20-25 minutes, until golden. Transfer to a wire rack to cool a little, although these are best enjoyed warm!

FIREWORK PINWHEELS

10+ months

PREP: 10–30 minutes

COOK: 60+ minutes

MAKES: about 24 pinwheels

¼ butternut squash, seeds
    scooped out
olive or sunflower oil,
    for roasting
1 garlic clove
1 tsp finely chopped
    rosemary
1 tsp finely chopped sage
100g cooked brown rice
50g cooked puy lentils
    (use from a can or pouch
    if you prefer)
30g (1oz) grated Parmesan
    cheese, vegetarian
    equivalent or pecorino
50g (2oz) soft goats' cheese
    (or any other soft cheese)
2 x 230g (8oz) packets of
    good-quality ready-rolled
    puff pastry
1 beaten egg (optional)

*see step 5

Take this fun treat along to a firework display or Bonfire night party! These pinwheels contain cooked rice so they should be eaten on the day they are made, either warm from the oven or cold later that day. Alternatively, they can be frozen once assembled (before cooking) and cooked straight from frozen; just cook them for slightly longer. For a simpler gluten-free option you can use damp hands to form the chilled filling into rounded discs, then brush with a little oil and bake for 20–30 minutes until golden.

1. Preheat the oven to 200°C/180°C fan/400°F/gas mark 6. Place the squash quarter in a roasting tray and drizzle with a little oil. Bash the garlic clove in its skin and add it to the roasting tray, then roast for about 45 minutes until soft.

2. Scoop the butternut squash out of its skin and into a large bowl. Squeeze the roasted garlic out of its skin and mash with the butternut squash. Stir in the rosemary and sage, followed by the rice and lentils.

3. Allow to cool slightly then add the two cheeses and mix thoroughly. Place in the fridge to chill completely.

4. When you are ready to assemble the pinwheels, preheat the oven to 200°C/180°C fan/400°F/gas mark 6. Unroll one of the packets of puff pastry on to a piece of baking parchment. Spread over half the chilled filling in a thin layer about 5mm (¼in) thick, leaving a 1cm (½in) border around the edge of the pastry. Carefully use the edge of the parchment to roll it up like a Swiss roll, then repeat with the second packet of pastry.

5. Cut each roll into slices 2cm (¾in) thick to create pinwheels – if you don't want to cook them all at once this is the point when you can freeze them, placing a sheet of baking parchment between each one. Otherwise cook and eat all of them on the same day.

6. Place the pinwheels on a greased baking sheet and brush with a little beaten egg, if using. Bake for about 30 minutes, or until golden and piping hot.

OMELETTE WHIRLS

10+ months

PREP: 10–20 minutes

COOK: under 10 minutes

MAKES: 1 large omelette or 8 whirls

2 large eggs
60ml (2fl oz/¼ cup) full-fat milk (or use a non-dairy alternative – water also works if you prefer)
½ small carrot, peeled and grated
½ small courgette (zucchini), grated
40g Cheddar cheese, grated
drizzle of vegetable oil, for cooking

This fun recipe is great for lunchboxes with some fresh salad and crudités; it's easy for little fingers to eat. You can use a dip or spread of your choice as an alternative to the cheese to hold the whirl together if you like, in which case remove the omelette from the pan before rolling up. These can be made in advance and kept in the fridge for up to 2 days; wrap in foil or put into plastic tubs for your little one's lunchbox.

1. In a bowl or jug whisk the eggs and milk, then stir in the grated vegetables and most of the cheese, reserving a small handful for later.

2. Heat a little oil in a large frying pan (skillet) over a medium heat then pour in the mixture and tip to cover the base of the pan. Cook for about 5 minutes until set and golden on the bottom, then use a fish slice to flip over and cook the other side. If you struggle to flip the large omelette over, you can cook the top under a warm grill (make sure your frying pan is ovenproof).

3. Turn off the heat then quickly spread the remaining grated cheese evenly over the omelette. The cheese should start to melt in the residual heat from the pan, so as this happens carefully roll the omelette up into a whirl, from one side of the pan to the other, taking care not to burn yourself on the hot pan. The melted cheese should hold the whirl together (add a little extra if needed). If the cheese isn't melting, then you can place the pan under a hot grill for a few seconds.

4. Remove the omelette from the pan and allow to cool. Once cool, cut the sausage-shaped whirl into slices about 1.5cm (½in) thick. Turn each one on to its side to see the whirl shapes and serve.

CARROT, CHICKPEA & MINT PATTIES

(V) (gf) ❄ *

PREP: 10–30 minutes

COOK: 25–35 minutes

MAKES: about 16–18 patties

FOR THE PATTIES:
**50g (2oz) cashews
(see page 7)
8 carrots, peeled and grated
400g (14oz) can chickpeas,
drained and rinsed
small bunch of fresh mint
small bunch of fresh coriander
100g (4oz) feta cheese
2 spring onions (scallions),
thinly sliced
2 tsp garam masala**

FOR THE TOMATO SALSA:
**4 tomatoes
10cm (4in) piece of cucumber
1 avocado, peeled and
stoned (optional)
handful of parsley leaves,
finely chopped
squeeze of lemon juice
splash of extra virgin olive oil**

TO SERVE:
**Little Gem lettuce leaves
Greek yoghurt
tahini (optional)**

*patties only

These little patties are like falafels but contain lots of healthy carrot and fresh mint for a different twist, making them delicious gluten-free lunchtime treats. They can be eaten hot or cold and are great for picnics. The patties keep in the fridge for up to 3 days. Avoid using cashews for very young babies, due to risk of choking.

1. Preheat the oven to 200°C/180°C fan/400°F/gas mark 6.

2. If using the cashews spread them out on a baking tray and pop into the oven to toast for 5–10 minutes (be careful not to burn them). Set aside.

3. Put the cashews into a food processor and blitz briefly. Add all the remaining patty ingredients and mix together using the pulse setting so that they come together to form a soft dough. Be careful not to over-mix as it will become too sticky. If you don't have a food processor, chop all the ingredients as finely as possible and mix together in a bowl. If the ingredients don't come together enough with this method, you can add just a little water.

4. Grease and line a couple of baking sheets with baking parchment. With slightly damp hands scoop out some of the mixture and press into little patties about 5cm (2in) across and 2cm (¾in) deep. Place on the lined baking sheets about 2cm (¾in) apart. You should get 16–18 patties. Bake for 20–25 minutes until golden.

5. Meanwhile, make the salsa. Finely chop the tomatoes, cucumber and avocado, if using, into tiny dice and put into a bowl. Add the parsley and lemon juice and a splash of good-quality olive oil.

6. To serve, place one patty into a Little Gem lettuce leaf, top with some Greek yoghurt, salsa and a drizzle of tahini, if liked.

TOP TIP: little babies may struggle with the lettuce wrap – so let them eat the patties separately and play with the yoghurt dip and salsa. Picking these up helps them build confidence and discover different food textures. You can help them at the end with a spoon if there's any left!

CAULIFLOWER COUSCOUS WITH ROAST VEG & TURMERIC CREAM

PREP: 10-30 minutes

COOK: 25-30 minutes

MAKES: 4 servings (as a side dish)

¼ cauliflower
1 red (bell) pepper, deseeded and cut into bite-sized pieces
½ aubergine (eggplant), cut into bite-sized pieces
2 courgettes (zucchini), cut into bite-sized pieces
1 sweet potato, peeled and cut into bite-sized pieces
1 red onion, roughly chopped
1 garlic clove
drizzle of vegetable oil or coconut oil
200ml coconut cream (or use single cream for a non-vegan alternative)
1 tsp turmeric
small handful of fresh coriander (cilantro) or herb of your choice, to serve (optional)

This vegtastic dish is bursting with colour and great ingredients! It's really easy to make, too, making it a perfect summer barbecue side dish. It's also delicious as a light lunch or snack.

1. Preheat the oven to 200°C/180°C fan/400°F/gas mark 6. Break the cauliflower into florets, then blitz in a food processor to make 'cauliflower couscous'. Set aside in a large bowl.

2. Tip all the vegetables into a roasting tray. Bash the garlic in its skin with the side of a knife and add to the roasting tray. Drizzle with a little oil and roast for 20-25 minutes (you could also cook this in a tray on the barbecue if you already have the barbecue lit).

3. Once nicely roasted, spoon out the hot vegetables and stir into the bowl of raw cauli couscous. Remove the garlic clove and set aside.

4. To make a simple sauce, add the coconut cream (or single cream if you prefer) and turmeric to the roasting tray and stir around to soak up the roasted vegetable flavours (a bit like making a gravy). Chop the roasted garlic clove and stir into the sauce. Heat the sauce through over the hob, on the barbecue or by placing back in the oven for a couple of minutes.

5. Pour the sauce over the couscous and vegetables then chop the fresh coriander and sprinkle over the top. This can be eaten hot or cold and you can mash the vegetables a little if you want a slightly softer texture.

BUTTERNUT SQUASH & PUY LENTIL SALAD WITH GOATS' CHEESE

PREP: 10-30 minutes

COOK: 25-30 minutes

MAKES: 2 adult and 1 baby portion

2 garlic cloves, unpeeled
½ butternut squash, peeled and cut into 1cm (½in) cubes
1 red onion, unpeeled and quartered
olive oil, for roasting
pinch of garam masala (optional)
90g puy lentils
90g quinoa
large handful of spinach, finely chopped
small handful of parsley leaves, finely chopped
75g (3oz) soft goats' cheese, crumbled

FOR THE TAHINI DRESSING:
4 tbsp tahini
2 tbsp olive oil
1 tbsp lemon juice
1 garlic clove, crushed (optional)

Sweet butternut squash is loved by most babies, which should make this dish a firm favourite! Try with a simple dressing or experiment with our tahini dressing; vegan or dairy-free babies will particularly benefit from the tahini dressing which is full of calcium. It also helps the salad stick together a little – which can make it easier for little ones to pick it up. The goats' cheese and soft squash can be mashed with the lentils and quinoa a little for young babies.

1. Preheat the oven to 200°C/180°C fan/400°F/gas mark 6.

2. Bash the garlic with the flat side of a knife and put it with the squash and onion into a small roasting tray. Drizzle with a little oil and sprinkle over the garam masala, if using. Roast for 20–25 minutes, or until nicely roasted.

3. In the meantime, cook the puy lentils and quinoa separately: bring two small pans of water to the boil while you rinse the lentils and quinoa. Add to each pan and simmer gently; the puy lentils take about 20 minutes and the quinoa about 15 minutes. They're cooked when the lentils are just soft, and the quinoa has opened into little spirals

4. Meanwhile, make the dressing by simply whisking all the ingredients together or shaking them together in a jar with a tight-fitting lid.

5. Drain the cooked lentils and quinoa and tip into a large serving bowl. Allow the roasted red onion to cool slightly, then peel and finely dice (chopping the onion after roasting it means no stinging eyes and it prevents the onion from burning in the oven). Add the onion and half the butternut squash to the bowl, discarding the garlic cloves – reserve the other half of the squash in a tub for another recipe (it will keep in fridge for up to 3 days, or can be frozen).

6. Stir through the spinach and parsley and pour over your chosen dressing. Finish by scattering over the crumbled goats' cheese. Serve warm or cold.

RAINBOW FRITTERS

   (V) (gf) (df) ❄

PREP: 10-30 minutes

COOK: 10-30 minutes

MAKES: 6-8 fritters

FOR THE BASIC BATTER:
1 egg
1 tbsp flour (gluten free if required)
oil, for frying

FOR THE VEGETABLES (CHOOSE ANY OF THE FOLLOWING):
sweetcorn
kale
spring onions (scallions)
peas
butternut squash
beetroot (beets)
celeriac (celery root)
swede
parsnip
potatoes
spinach

OPTIONAL EXTRAS:
grated or crumbled cheese
fresh or dried herbs
sautéed onion and garlic
spices

These make great finger food for little ones and are easy to make with whatever seasonal vegetables you have – see below for some ideas. Serve with a salad or some steamed greens as part of a meal, or as a nutritious snack on their own or with a dip such as hummous or guacamole. They keep well in the fridge for a couple of days.

1. Make a batter in a large bowl by whisking the egg and flour together.

2. Prepare your chosen seasonal vegetable. Root vegetables are best par-boiled, cooled, then grated. Leafy vegetables can be shredded very finely and mixed in raw, although kale is quite a tough green and may benefit from being steamed very lightly first. We use a handful of sweetcorn (yellow), a handful of kale, chopped spring onions and peas (green), a handful of grated butternut squash (orange) and a handful of grated beetroot (red), to make eight fritters.

3. Divide your batter if making more than one colour, then stir your prepared vegetables into the batter and add any herbs or extras of your choice.

4. Heat a little oil in a large frying pan (skillet) over a medium heat. Add a spoonful of the vegetable batter and gently spread to create a little circular fritter about 6cm (2½in) across (you should be able to fit about 4 fritters in your pan at a time). Cook over a medium heat for about 5 minutes, then carefully turn over with a fish slice and cook the other side until golden and cooked through.

5. You can keep the cooked fritters warm in a low oven while you cook the rest; this also helps to cook the fritter through.

6. The fritters are delicious eaten warm or cold and can easily be reheated in the oven.

FLAVOUR COMBINATION IDEAS:
Kale, pea, mint, spring onion and goats' cheese / Beetroot (beet), thyme and feta / Squash, onion, garlic and sage / Sweetcorn and Cheddar with dried herbs / Grated courgette (zucchini) with mint and feta

VEGETABLE BREAD

12+ months

PREP: 60 minutes

COOK: 60+ minutes

MAKES: about 4 servings

2 medium courgettes (zucchini), grated

100g (4oz) carrot, peeled and grated

2 tbsp olive oil

1 small red onion, finely chopped

350g (12oz/3 cups) plain or wholemeal flour, plus extra for dusting

7g (¼oz) fast-action dried yeast

2 tbsp fresh basil, finely chopped

125ml (4fl oz/½ cup) tepid water

A great addition to any mealtime. You can also try using different veggies if your little one has a favourite or if you fancy adding your own twist.

1. After grating the courgette and carrot place in a colander set over a sink to allow the excess water to drain away. If still very wet, pat dry with kitchen paper (paper towels) or a clean tea towel.

2. Heat 1 tablespoon of the olive oil in a frying pan (skillet) and cook the onion over a low–medium heat for 5–10 minutes, until softened. Add the courgette and carrot, increase the heat to medium and cook until tender, about 2–3 minutes. Try to cook off the water so the vegetables are dry. Remove from the heat and leave to cool, then strain any excess water.

3. Mix together the flour and yeast in a bowl then add the vegetables, basil and remaining tablespoon of oil. Mix well, then stir in the warm water. When the dough starts to come together use your hands to bring the ingredients into a ball.

4. Lightly dust your work surface with flour then tip the dough on to it and knead for 10 minutes. Shape the dough into a ball, place in a lightly oiled bowl and cover with a piece of lightly oiled cling film (plastic wrap) to stop the dough sticking to it.

5. Leave the dough to prove in a warm place for 30 minutes, or until the dough has doubled in size. Meanwhile, preheat the oven to 220°C/200°C fan/425°F/gas mark 7.

6. When ready to bake, remove the dough from the bowl and shape into an oval loaf shape. Place on an oiled baking tray and bake in the oven for 40 minutes, until golden. Test the bread by tapping the bottom – if it sounds hollow, it's ready.

7. Leave to cool on a wire rack before slicing and serving.

RAINBOW WRAPS

PREP: 30-45 minutes

COOK: about 20 minutes

MAKES: 4-6 portions

FOR THE WRAPS:
100g (4oz) buckwheat flour
1 egg
300ml (10fl oz/1¼ cups)
milk (or use a rice/oat/
nut milk alternative)
3 tbsp water
olive or coconut oil,
for frying

FOR THE RAINBOW FILLING:
½ cooked beetroot (beets)
¼ red (bell) pepper
1 small carrot
¼ yellow pepper
5cm (2in) chunk of cucumber
2-3 tbsp cream cheese
or hummous

All the colours! Our tasty veggie wraps are a great alternative to boring sarnies in the lunchbox or a handy packed lunch when you're out for the day.

1. To make the wrap, simply whisk all the ingredients (except the oil) together until very smooth (ideally use an electric whisk, if you have one). Allow the batter to stand for about half an hour.

2. Heat a little olive or coconut oil in a 15cm (6in) non-stick frying pan (skillet). Ladle a scoop of batter into the pan – just enough to cover the pan surface, so the wrap is no thicker than 5mm (¼in). Tilt the pan so the batter covers the surface and allow to cook over a medium heat for a couple of minutes.

3. Use a fish slice to carefully see if it is cooked on the bottom. Once it's cooked on one side, slide the fish slice under the wrap and flip it over. Cook the other side for a couple more minutes, until golden. Transfer to a wire rack and repeat with the rest of the mixture – you should get 4-6 wraps. Allow the wraps to cool on the wire rack, or, if you prefer them warm, they can be kept warm in a low oven.

4. Prepare all the filling vegetables by cutting them into thin matchsticks; the carrot and beetroot could also be grated if preferred.

5. Spread a layer of cream cheese or hummous over the whole wrap. Place the vegetables on top of the wrap in strips arranged by colour. Fold up the top and bottom of the wrap, then tightly roll, spreading a little extra cheese or hummous on the last bit of wrap to help 'glue' it in place if needed.

6. Slice in half at an angle so that you can see the range of rainbow colours.

NOTE: To make this quicker and simpler you could simply use shop-bought wraps (check the ingredients and be aware these may not be gluten free). If you make them yourself any leftover wraps can used the next day or frozen – layer baking parchment between each wrap before freezing.

SWEETCORN CAKES

PREP: under 10 minutes

COOK: 10–20 minutes

MAKES: about 12 cakes

200g (7oz) can sweetcorn, drained
1 garlic clove, finely chopped
½ small red onion, finely chopped
2 tbsp ground coriander
100g (4oz/1 cup) plain flour
2 large eggs
vegetable oil, for frying
freshly ground black pepper

A tasty toddler snack or side dish that's great served with a topping of your choice. Cut into fingers for little ones to grab hold!

1. Put half the sweetcorn into a blender and blitz until smooth. Add the garlic, onion, coriander and some freshly ground black pepper and blitz to a purée.

2. Add the flour and eggs then blend for another minute. Scrape the mixture into a bowl and fold through the remaining sweetcorn.

3. Heat a little oil in a frying pan (skillet), drop a spoonful of the batter into the pan and repeat until you have 3–4 patties frying at once.

4. Once golden on one side, flip over and cook the other side until golden. Remove from the pan and keep warm while you cook the remaining cakes.

OATY APPLE, RAISIN & WENSLEYDALE MUFFINS

PREP: 10–30 minutes

COOK: 20–30 minutes

MAKES: 12 muffins

6 tbsp sunflower oil
2 large eggs
250ml (8fl oz/1 cup) fresh apple juice
150g (5oz/generous 1 cup) self-raising flour
1½ tsp baking powder
150g (5oz/¾ cup) rolled oats
75g raisins
80g (3oz) Wensleydale cheese, grated
200g (7oz) Cox apples, peeled, cored and coarsely grated

A tasty sweet and savoury muffin recipe, packed full of nutritious ingredients for your toddler to explore. Great for a lunchbox or picnic.

1. Preheat the oven to 200°C/180°C fan/400°F/gas mark 6 and line a 12-hole muffin tin (pan) with 12 paper cases.

2. Put the oil, eggs and apple juice into a large jug or bowl and beat lightly to combine.

3. Sift together the flour and baking powder in a large bowl, then add the oats, raisins, 60g (2½oz) of the grated cheese and the grated apple. Mix together thoroughly.

4. Make a well in the centre of the dry ingredients and pour in the liquid mixture. Stir together gently until just combined; don't over-mix.

5. Spoon the mixture evenly into the muffin cases and then sprinkle the remaining cheese on top. Bake in the oven for about 20 minutes, or until risen, golden brown and firm to the touch.

6. Leave to cool in the tin for about 5 minutes, then either serve warm or transfer to a wire rack to cool completely.

SPINACH & MUSHROOM PANCAKES

PREP: 30–60 minutes

COOK: 15–25 minutes

MAKES: 4 adult and 2 toddler pancakes

FOR THE PANCAKE BATTER:
150g (5oz/generous 1 cup) plain flour
2 eggs
250ml milk
1 tbsp rapeseed or vegetable oil
50g (2oz) spinach

FOR THE MUSHROOM FILLING:
rapeseed or vegetable oil, for frying
½ small onion, diced
1 garlic clove, crushed
500g (1lb 2oz) mixed mushrooms, chopped
2 tbsp chopped fresh tarragon
2 tbsp chopped fresh parsley
1 tsp dried thyme
juice of ½ lemon

FOR THE RICOTTA TOPPING (OPTIONAL):
250g ricotta
grated zest of 1 lemon and juice of ½

Bright and colourful, these pancakes filled with sautéed mushrooms make the perfect family lunch or dinner. To make this dairy-free, you can skip the ricotta topping and make the batter with a milk alternative.

1. Whisk the flour, eggs, milk and oil together in a large bowl until you have a smooth batter. Transfer to a blender with the spinach and blitz until smooth. Leave to rest for 30 minutes.

2. Meanwhile, make the filling. Heat a little oil in a large frying pan (skillet). Add the diced onion and fry over a medium heat until soft. Add the garlic, mushrooms and herbs to the pan and continue to cook for 10–15 minutes, until soft. Stir often so that the mushrooms do not stick to the bottom of the pan. When they are done, remove from the heat and stir in the lemon juice. Keep warm in a low oven.

3. In a small bowl, mix ricotta with the lemon zest and juice of the remaining lemon half. Set aside.

4. Place a medium crêpe/frying pan (skillet) over a medium–high heat. Wipe it with some greased kitchen paper (paper towels). Add a ladleful of the spinach batter to the pan and allow it to spread evenly. When small bubbles appear on the surface of the pancake it is ready to flip; turn over and cook it on the other side. Set aside in a warm oven while you cook the remaining pancakes, using half a ladleful of spinach batter mix to make toddler-sized pancakes.

5. Serve the pancakes filled with the mushroom mixture and with a dollop of ricotta on the side.

NO-JUNK SCOTCH EGGS

PREP: 30-60 minutes

COOK: 30-40 minutes

MAKES: 4 Scotch eggs

6 eggs
200g lean sausage meat
200g lean turkey mince
1 tbsp English mustard
1 tbsp dried mixed herbs
½ tsp freshly grated nutmeg
45g (1½oz) plain flour
75g (3oz) breadcrumbs
spray oil

Baked instead of fried and using half sausage meat and half lean turkey mince, these healthier Scotch eggs are ideal for a picnic. You can swap the turkey mince for chicken mince. Make sure you use good-quality sausage meat that is at least 95 per cent meat. Eat these warm or cold with your favourite condiments.

1. Put 4 of the eggs into a pan of cold water and place over a high heat. As soon as the water comes to the bowl, reduce the heat slightly and cook the eggs for 5-6 minutes. Drain and refill the pan with cold water; leave the eggs in the water to cool. Once cooled, peel the eggs and set aside.

2. While the eggs are cooking, mix together the sausage meat, turkey mince, mustard, mixed herbs and nutmeg.

3. Cut one large square of cling film (plastic wrap) and put a quarter of the meat mix in the middle. Cover it with another large square of cling film and then flatten with a rolling pin to an even thickness of 5mm (¼in).

4. Remove the top layer of cling film. Place one egg in the middle of the meat and carefully roll the meat around the egg using the bottom layer of cling film to help you. Shape the meat evenly and tightly around the egg with your hands, removing any excess meat mixture. Place the egg on a plate and repeat with the remaining 3 eggs and meat mixture (you can reuse the cling film squares). Once finished, put the eggs in the fridge to chill for 15 minutes.

5. Preheat the oven to 200°C/180°C fan/400°F/gas mark 6 and line a baking tray with baking parchment. Place the baking tray in front of you, along with 3 bowls: one for the flour, one for the remaining 2 eggs, beaten, and one for the breadcrumbs.

6. Coat each Scotch egg first in flour, then in the beaten eggs, and finally in the breadcrumbs. Add another layer of breadcrumbs by rolling each egg again in the beaten egg and breadcrumbs.

7. Place the Scotch eggs on the lined baking tray and spray with oil. Bake for 25-30 minutes, until golden. Serve warm or cold with salad and condiments.

SWEET POTATO & GOATS' CHEESE MINI QUICHES

12+ months

PREP: 40–60 minutes

COOK: 60+ minutes

MAKES: 6 mini quiches

FOR THE PASTRY:
150g (5oz) unsalted butter, diced
300g (10oz/2¼ cups) plain flour
about 3 tbsp cold water

Great finger food for little ones with lots of healthy vegetables and calcium-rich cheese – these can be served as frittatas without the pastry. To make frittatas you can very simply put all of the ingredients straight into a well-greased muffin tin without the pastry.

1. Rub the butter into the flour with your fingertips (or use a food processor, using the 'pulse' button). The secret is not to over-handle the butter and flour; keep the touch very light, until you have a crumb consistency.

2. Now add a little of the water and start to press the crumbs together to form a dough in your bowl. Add a little more water and continue to bring together but be careful not to add too much. Massage the dough lightly, until you have one smooth ball of dough (do not over-work it). Wrap the dough in a clean plastic bag and put into the fridge for at least 30 minutes while you prepare the vegetables and preheat the oven to 200°C/180°C fan/400°F/gas mark 6.

3. Slice the leeks in half lengthways to create two semi-circular lengths, then cut these lengths into thick slices. Place the vegetables on to a lightly greased baking tray, and drizzle with oil. Bake for about 20 minutes, until nicely roasted, checking halfway through and giving a quick stir.

4. Meanwhile, prepare the pastry cases. Lightly flour a clean work surface and your rolling pin. Roll out the rested dough, turning it by 90 degrees after each roll to create an even circular sheet of pastry about 5mm (¼in) thick. Add extra flour to the surface as you roll, to stop the dough from sticking.

5. Cut around a saucer (or something similar) to create circles of pastry to fit a large 6-hole muffin tin (pan). Grease the tin very well with oil or butter and carefully press the pastry circles into the tin, cutting off any excess pastry and pressing the seams together to seal any gaps (any leftover pastry can be frozen and used another time).

FOR THE FILLING:
2 leeks, trimmed
2 sweet potatoes, peeled
    and cut into bite-sized
    cubes
good drizzle of olive oil
75g (3oz) soft goats' cheese
75g (3oz) Parmesan cheese
    or vegetarian equivalent,
    grated
6 eggs
300ml (10fl oz/1¼ cups)
    full-fat milk (or use a
    dairy-free alternative)
freshly ground black pepper

6. Blind-bake your pastry before adding the filling. Line each pastry case with a circle of baking parchment and fill with baking beans to weigh the paper down and keep the pastry flat. Pop into the oven for about 15 minutes, until the edges of the pastry are just starting to turn slightly golden. Remove the parchment and beans and return to the oven for a further 5 minutes, just to dry out the inside base of the pastry case. Remove from the oven and set aside.

7. Once cooled slightly, evenly distribute your cooked veg between the pastry cases, crumble in the goats' cheese and add the Parmesan and a grind of black pepper.

8. Whisk the eggs and milk together thoroughly in a jug, then pour into each hole over the filling, making sure you don't fill right to the top.

9. Carefully transfer to the oven and bake for 20 minutes, or until golden and set. Allow them to cool in the tin, then carefully ease out with a palette knife.

Dinner

PARSNIP & BUTTERNUT SQUASH PURÉE

   (v) (gf) (df) ❄

PREP: under 10 minutes

COOK: 20–30 minutes

MAKES: lots of portions – ideal for freezing in ice-cube trays for weaning

1 parsnip, peeled and thickly sliced
half a medium butternut squash, peeled, deseeded and thickly sliced
a little water (if needed)

The natural sweetness of parsnip and butternut squash make this a great first weaning purée for when you want to introduce your little one to some different veg.

1. Steam the parsnips until soft, 20–30 minutes, either using a steamer or by placing the parsnips in a colander over a pan of simmering water and covering (you could boil the parsnips instead, if you prefer).

2. In a bowl, blend the parsnips to a smooth purée, adding some water if required – just enough to get the right consistency. A hand blender will give the smoothest texture, but a food processor or blender can also be used.

3. For an even smoother texture, push the purée through a fine sieve.

CARROT, RED LENTIL & GARAM MASALA PURÉE

   (v) (gf) (df) ❄

PREP: under 10 minutes

COOK: 20–30 minutes

MAKES: lots of portions – ideal for freezing in ice-cube trays for weaning

2 carrots, peeled and thickly sliced
50g red lentils, rinsed
1 tsp garam masala

This purée is a more filling meal for your little ones, as the lentils provide lots of healthy protein. The garam masala adds spice without heat so is a great way to introduce your baby to new flavours.

1. Place the carrots and red lentils in a pan, cover with cold water and bring to the boil. Reduce the heat to a simmer and cook for about 20 minutes until both the carrots and lentils are tender.

2. Remove from the heat, add the garam masala and use a hand blender to blitz until smooth (or use a food processor).

TOP TIP: this purée can be watered down into a soup, or it can be enjoyed cold as a dip with veg sticks – tasty!

gf

PREP: 10-15 minutes

COOK: 15-25 minutes

MAKES: 3-4 portions

olive oil, for frying
50g (2oz) chicken breast, cut
 into chunks
1 carrot, peeled and diced
1 sweet potato, peeled and
 diced
3 asparagus spears, trimmed
30g (1oz) Cheddar cheese,
 grated

A tasty mash using sweet potato and cheese, which introduces the delicious taste of asparagus. You can use scissors to chop the ingredients to a more manageable but still chunky texture, or mash for a softer texture. For an early weaning purée blend the mixture until smooth.

1. Heat a drizzle of oil in a frying pan (skillet) and sauté the chicken pieces over a medium-high heat for about 8–10 minutes, turning frequently. Check it is cooked all the way through.

2. Chop the cooked chicken into even smaller pieces, about 1cm (½in).

3. Steam the carrot and sweet potato for about 10 minutes, until soft, then add the asparagus for an additional 4 minutes (you can boil the vegetables instead if you prefer).

4. Mix all these cooked ingredients together with the cheese and allow the cheese to melt.

SHEPHERD'S PIE

PREP: 10–30 minutes

COOK: 60+ minutes

MAKES: 4 adult and
1 baby portion

500g minced lamb
olive oil, for frying
1 onion, finely chopped
2 carrots, peeled and diced
2 celery sticks, finely
  chopped
2 garlic cloves, crushed
400g (14oz) can chopped
  tomatoes
small handful of fresh thyme
  leaves
pinch of black pepper
500ml (16fl oz/2 cups) hot
  water or homemade stock
  (ideally homemade with
  no added salt, or a low salt
  alternative)

FOR THE MASH:
800g floury potatoes,
  peeled and cut into chunks
1 tbsp unsalted butter
  (optional)
2 eggs, beaten (optional)

This is a classic dish that all the family will love. What's more it can easily be made in advance and heated through the next day. If heating from cold, cover with foil and heat for 30 minutes, then remove the foil for an additional 10 minutes to brown the potato top. Serve with broccoli 'trees'. Make sure you allow to cool before serving to baby.

1. Preheat the oven to 200°C/180°C fan/400°F/gas mark 6.

2. First fry the minced lamb for just a couple of minutes in a lidded casserole without any added oil. You don't want the meat to sweat, so fry in small batches, removing the browned meat to a sieve over a bowl as soon as it's coloured. The sieve allows any excess fat or water to drain.

3. Wipe the casserole clean with some kitchen paper (paper towels) and add a splash of olive oil. Sauté the onion, carrots and celery over a low heat for about 10 minutes, until soft. Add the garlic and cook for another minute.

4. Return the meat to the casserole along with the canned tomatoes, thyme leaves, black pepper and hot water or stock and stir well. Cover with the lid and transfer to the oven for about 1 hour, checking and stirring halfway through the cooking time.

5. After half an hour you can start preparing the potato topping. Put the potatoes into a pan of cold water and bring to the boil. Cook for about 20 minutes until tender. Drain and mash with the butter and beaten egg, if using. The eggs give the potato a wonderful golden crust when baked but can be left out if you prefer.

6. When the lamb is cooked, remove the casserole from the oven and carefully spread the mashed potato over the cooked meat; fork over the top. Return to the oven for another 20–30 minutes without the lid until the potato is golden and the filling is piping hot. Cool a little before serving and mash or blend to a consistency that's right for your little one.

RATATOUILLE

PREP: 10-20 minutes

COOK: 15-25 minutes

MAKES: 3-4 portions

1 tbsp olive oil
1 red onion, diced
1 garlic clove, crushed
½ red (bell) pepper, diced
½ yellow (bell) pepper, diced
½ small courgette (zucchini),
 diced
½ aubergine (eggplant),
 diced
sprig of fresh thyme
1 bay leaf
2 large tomatoes, diced

A versatile recipe that is great for the whole family. For toddlers and the rest of the family serve the ratatouille as a sauce over wholegrain pasta with a sprinkling of grated cheese or serve with grilled chicken and some homemade bread.

1. Heat the olive oil in a pan, add the onion and garlic and cook together over a low heat for about 10 minutes until softened.

2. Add the diced pepper, courgette and aubergine with the thyme and bay leaf and leave to cook until the vegetables begin to soften.

3. Add the tomatoes and continue to cook until the vegetables are tender. Add a little water if the dish starts to dry out.

4. Remove the thyme and bay leaf before serving. Purée the ratatouille to a suitable consistency for your little one. Once your baby is used to the texture you can mash or chop it rather than puréeing.

VEGETARIAN IRISH STEW

PREP: 10-30 minutes

COOK: 60+ minutes

MAKES: 2 adult and 2 baby portions

1 tbsp vegetable oil
½ onion, chopped
1 celery stick, chopped
2–3 tbsp pearl barley
sprig of thyme
1 bay leaf
pinch of black pepper
500ml (16fl oz/2 cups)
    vegetable stock (ideally
    homemade with no
    added salt, or a low salt
    alternative)
2 carrots, peeled and cut
    into chunks
2 medium potatoes, peeled
    and cut into chunks
¼ swede, peeled and cut
    into chunks
2 tbsp quinoa
80g (3oz) kale or spring
    greens

A tasty veggie option that can be served to babies and toddlers – delicious served with some freshly baked bread.

1. Heat the oil in a heavy-based pan or casserole, add the onion and celery and fry gently for 3 minutes.

2. Add the barley, thyme, bay leaf, black pepper and vegetable stock and bring to the boil. Reduce the heat to medium, cover and cook for 1 hour, stirring occasionally.

3. After 1 hour, add the carrots, potatoes, swede and quinoa and cook until tender, about 15–20 minutes (top up with more water if the pan looks dry).

4. Add the kale or spring greens and cook for a further 5 minutes to wilt down.

5. Serve as it is for toddlers, breaking up any larger chunks, or mash or blend to a suitable texture for younger babies.

BABY FISH PIE

PREP: under 10 minutes

COOK: 15–25 minutes

MAKES: 4 portions

200g (7oz) line-caught white
   fish fillet (such as haddock
   or cod)
1 bay leaf
300ml (10fl oz/1¼ cups) milk
300g (10oz) potatoes,
   peeled and diced
100g (4oz) frozen peas
2 tsp chopped fresh parsley

This delicious fish recipe for little ones is one of our most popular weaning recipes – why not give it a try?

1. Place the fish in a frying pan (skillet) with the bay leaf, pour over the milk and poach over a low heat for 5–10 minutes, or until the fish is cooked. Lift the fish out with a slotted spoon and remove all the skin and any bones. Strain the poaching liquid and set aside.

2. Cook the potatoes in a pan of boiling water for about 12 minutes, until cooked. Add the peas to the pan for the final few minutes of cooking, so they are cooked but still nice and green.

3. Drain the potato and peas, flake the fish with a fork, then place everything in a bowl with the chopped parsley.

4. Purée until smooth or mash to the desired texture – add the poaching liquid to soften the mixture and achieve the right consistency for your little one.

SLOW-COOKED BEEF STEW

PREP: 10-30 minutes

COOK: 60+ minutes

MAKES: 2 adult and
2-3 baby portions

FOR THE STEW:
**400g (14oz) beef stewing
steak, cut into 2cm (¾in)
cubes**
1 onion, roughly chopped
1½ tsp ground cinnamon
a few grinds of black pepper
**320ml (10fl oz/1¼ cups)
water**
**2 sweet potatoes
(300g/10oz), peeled and
cut into 2cm (¾in) cubes**

FOR THE MASH:
**6 medium new potatoes
(400g/14oz), quartered**
**2 carrots, peeled and cut
into thick slices**
**½ celeriac, peeled and
cut into chunks**

**A winter warmer for the whole family to enjoy; this beef stew can be
served as it is for adults and toddlers and should be soft enough to mash
for babies from 10 months. Otherwise use a hand blender to purée the
food to the right texture for babies from 7 months.**

1. Preheat the oven to 160°C/140°C fan/325°F/gas mark 3. Choose an ovenproof
   dish with a tight-fitting lid that will hold the beef in no more than 2 layers.

2. Put the diced beef, onion, cinnamon, black pepper and water into the
   ovenproof dish and add the lid (or cover with foil).

3. Slow-cook for 3 hours. Check and stir the stew halfway through the cooking
   time and make sure there is enough water just covering the beef (top up
   with more water if needed).

4. After 3 hours, add the sweet potato and cook for a further 45-55 minutes,
   until the sweet potato is tender.

5. Half an hour before the stew is ready, prepare the mash. Put the potatoes
   into a pan of cold water and bring to the boil; cook for 10 minutes. Add the
   carrots and celeriac to the potatoes and boil for a further 20 minutes, or until
   the vegetables are tender.

6. Mash the vegetables to the required consistency and serve with the
   beef stew.

VEGETABLE & COCONUT KORMA

PREP: 10–30 minutes

COOK: 30–40 minutes

MAKES: 2 adult and
1 baby portion

1 tsp cumin seeds
1 tsp coriander seeds
1 tbsp vegetable oil
1 onion, finely chopped
2 garlic cloves, finely
   chopped
2cm (¾in) piece of fresh
   ginger, peeled and grated
   (optional)
½ tsp ground turmeric
1 tsp garam masala
½ butternut squash, peeled
   and diced
5 mushrooms, chopped
400ml (14fl oz) can coconut
   milk
100g (4oz) frozen peas
cooked brown basmati rice,
   to serve
chopped fresh coriander
   (cilantro), to garnish

This classic korma is a great way to introduce your children to gentle Indian spices. Use whichever vegetables are in season, always adding any quick cooking greens at the end as they cook the fastest.

1. Using a pestle and mortar, crush the cumin and coriander seeds to a coarse powder (or use ready-ground spices if you prefer).

2. Heat the oil in a pan with a lid, then add the onion and sauté over a low-medium heat until soft. Add the garlic, ginger, if using, and ground spices. Fry, stirring, for another minute.

3. Add the butternut squash, mushrooms and coconut milk and simmer with the lid on for 10 minutes, then with the lid off for a further 10 minutes until the squash is tender and the sauce has reduced a little. Add the peas and cook for another 3 minutes.

4. Serve with some cooked brown basmati rice and a sprinkle of fresh coriander. You can mash or blend to a smoother texture for a younger baby.

MEDITERRANEAN CHICKEN

PREP: under 10 minutes

COOK: 30–40 minutes

MAKES: 4–5 portions

1 courgette (zucchini),
   thickly sliced
1 red (bell) pepper,
   deseeded and cut into
   chunks
about 20 cherry tomatoes,
   halved
olive oil, for roasting
dried oregano or mixed
   herbs (optional)
½ cooked chicken breast

Simple and delicious roasted veggies and chicken, this is a winner for the whole family. If you heat the chicken separately then you can mash or blend the remaining roasted vegetables and use as a sauce for pasta or potatoes. This can be served to the rest of the family, perhaps with more cooked chicken.

1. Preheat the oven to 200°C/180°C fan/400°F/gas mark 6.

2. Put the courgette, pepper and tomatoes into a roasting tray, drizzle with a little olive oil, sprinkle with the dried herbs, if using, and roast for 30–40 minutes until nicely cooked.

3. Cut the cooked chicken into bite-sized pieces, then add to the roasting tray for the last 10 minutes of cooking – make sure the chicken is piping hot.

4. Mix everything together. This can be served chunky as it is for older children or mashed or blended to a suitable consistency for younger babies.

PREP: 10–30 minutes

COOK: 60+ minutes

MAKES: 2 adult and
2 baby portions

large knob of butter
drizzle of olive oil
8 sage leaves, finely
 shredded
2 onions, finely chopped
2 celery sticks, finely chopped
1 large leek, finely chopped
2 garlic cloves, crushed
1 tsp garam masala
 (optional)
½ butternut squash or other
 sweet seasonal squash,
 peeled and cut into 1cm
 (½in) dice
½ swede, peeled and cut
 into 1cm (½in) dice
100g (4oz) green lentils
500ml (16fl oz/2 cups) hot
 vegetable stock (ideally
 homemade with no
 added salt, or a low salt
 alternative)
cooked brown rice, to serve

This is ideal for when you need a hearty, winter dish that will give you a comforting 'food hug' on a cold day!

1. Gently heat the butter and oil in a large casserole over a low–medium heat and add the sage. Allow the sage to infuse its delicious flavour into the butter for a couple of minutes, but don't let it burn.

2. Add the onions, celery, leek, garlic and garam masala, if using, to the casserole and sauté gently until soft (the garam masala is optional but it adds a lovely depth of flavour to the dish).

3. Add the diced vegetables and stir. Rinse the lentils thoroughly and add to the pot with the hot stock. Everything should be submerged (if not, add a little extra stock or water).

4. Bring to a gentle boil, then reduce to a low simmer and cook with a lid on for 30 minutes, then without the lid for another 30 minutes, or until the liquid has reduced and become thick.

5. Serve the stew with some brown rice, for the perfect combination. The stew can be mashed or puréed for younger babies if they prefer.

PREP: 10–20 minutes

COOK: 30–60 minutes

MAKES: 2 adult and 1 baby portion (with tomato sauce to keep for next time)

olive or coconut oil, for frying
1 onion, very finely chopped
1 celery stick, very finely
    chopped
1 garlic clove, crushed
400g (14oz) can chopped
    tomatoes
1 tbsp tomato purée
2 tsp mixed dried herbs
large handful of carrots,
    peeled and finely chopped
large handful of leeks, finely
    chopped
170g (6oz) pasta (gluten-
    free pasta can be used)
grated Cheddar or Parmesan
    cheese or vegetarian
    equivalent, to serve
    (optional)

*sauce only

A classic no-fail recipe that's so easy to throw together. We used carrots and leeks, but you can use any seasonal veg you like, such as peas, broccoli or red pepper (but not potatoes as these are too starchy). Try adding some hot cooked fish or meat for added protein and serve alongside some fresh green leaves. Some crushed pine nuts or seeds make a good vegan alternative to cheese to finish off the dish. You will probably have some tomato sauce left; it can be kept in the fridge for up to 3 days or frozen for another meal.

1. Heat a splash of oil in a pan, add the onion and celery and sauté over a low–medium heat for about 5 minutes, until soft. Add the garlic and cook for another minute.

2. Add the chopped tomatoes, tomato purée and herbs and cook for about 10 minutes until the flavour intensifies. This makes the basic tomato sauce, which can be blended to a smooth consistency or left chunky.

3. Meanwhile steam the carrots for about 20 minutes, adding the leeks for the final 5 minutes of the cooking time.

4. Cook the pasta according to the instructions on the packet, then drain.

5. Drain the steamed vegetables and serve over the freshly cooked pasta with as much of the tomato sauce as you like. Add some grated cheese to serve, if liked.

NOTE: you can mash or blend the carrots and leeks into the sauce for a smoother texture, or even blend the entire dish into a purée for younger babies if you like. Adjust the consistency until just right for your little one.

Small 'baby' pasta shapes can be used if your little one prefers to eat with a spoon. Alternatively, some babies like to pick up regular-sized fusilli or penne with their fingers and take a bite… try both and see which they prefer.

COURGETTE PESTO SPAGHETTI

PREP: 10–30 minutes

COOK: under 10 minutes

MAKES: 2 adult and
1 baby portion

2 courgettes (zucchini),
   trimmed
about 8–10 cherry
   tomatoes, diced
½ ripe avocado, diced

FOR THE HOMEMADE
   PESTO:
50g (2oz/½ cup) pine nuts
   (see note below)
30g (1oz) Parmesan cheese
   or vegetarian equivalent
large handful of fresh basil
   leaves
100ml (3½fl oz/scant ½ cup)
   olive oil, plus more to
   loosen if needed
juice of 1 lemon (pips
   carefully discarded)
1–2 garlic cloves, depending
   on taste

Our very own courgette recipe is a great gluten-free spaghetti alternative. It's delicious served on its own or on top of bruschetta. To make some bruschetta simply rub half a garlic clove over a freshly toasted slice of baguette (or gluten-free bread of your choice), so that the garlic juice gently flavours the bruschetta. Give these to your little one to nibble on, or top with the courgette spaghetti and serve. A toasted baguette may be a bit challenging for younger babies, so ensure the texture is suitable. For small babies cut the spaghetti up into little bite-sized pieces to avoid choking. If you're trying baby-led weaning (BLW) babies will enjoy getting their fingers into this, or you can use a spoon too.

1. First make the pesto. Blitz all the ingredients together in a food processor or combine with a pestle and mortar. Set aside.

2. Use a julienne peeler to create courgette spaghetti (these are available cheaply from most kitchen shops). If you don't have a julienne peeler you can create courgette ribbons with an ordinary peeler, and then slice them into thinner strips for younger babies, or you can grate the courgettes. For young babies chop the courgette spaghetti into bite-sized pieces so that they are easier to eat.

3. The courgette spaghetti can be served raw or gently steamed for 2 minutes if younger babies prefer it softer. Combine the pesto with the spaghetti, tomatoes and avocado and serve cold, or this can be very gently warmed through in a pan if you prefer.

NOTE: pine nuts are not actually nuts but seeds; however, you may want to seek advice from your doctor before giving these to little ones if you have a history of nut allergies in your family.

SQUASH, MUSHROOM & SPINACH LASAGNE

PREP: 30–60 minutes

COOK: 60+ minutes

MAKES: about 6 servings

½ medium butternut squash, peeled and diced

vegetable oil, for cooking

4 large flat mushrooms, sliced

2 garlic cloves, crushed

10 fresh sage leaves, 5 chopped and 5 left whole

8 cooked, peeled chestnuts, chopped (see page 7; optional)

2 large handfuls of spinach leaves

½ onion, peeled

350ml (12fl oz/1½ cups) milk

25g (1oz) unsalted butter

25g (1 oz) plain flour (or use a gluten-free alternative)

50g (2oz) Parmesan cheese or vegetarian equivalent, grated

about 8 lasagne sheets (use gluten-free lasagne if required)

50g (2oz) goats' cheese or feta cheese (pasteurised)

A festive twist on a classic family favourite with chestnuts and sage to make a rich and filling veggie dinner. Serve with a fresh green salad or some cooked vegetables.

1. Preheat the oven to 200°C/180°C fan/400°F/gas mark 6. Tip the diced butternut squash into a small roasting tray, drizzle with a little oil and roast for about 25 minutes, until golden.

2. Heat a little oil in a frying pan (skillet) then sauté the mushrooms, garlic and chopped sage leaves for about 5 minutes until soft. Add the chestnuts to the pan with the spinach and cook for another minute, until the spinach wilts down. Tip into a bowl and set aside.

3. Add the onion half to a small pan with the milk and the whole sage leaves. Heat until the milk has just come to a gentle boil, then turn off the heat, cover with a lid and leave for 10 minutes to allow the milk to infuse with the flavour of the onion and sage. Strain the flavoured milk into a jug, discarding the herbs and onion.

4. To make the béchamel sauce, wipe out the pan, add the butter and flour to it and place over a low heat. Stir to form a paste (roux), then gradually whisk in the milk until a sauce forms. If you get any lumps just whisk vigorously until you have a smooth sauce. Remove from the heat and whisk in most of the grated Parmesan.

5. Pour a little sauce into the bottom of a 30 x 20cm (12 x 8in) lasagne dish, then add 2 sheets of lasagne, or enough to cover the base. Add a little more sauce, then a layer of the mushroom and spinach mixture. Scatter over some of the roasted butternut squash and some crumbled goats' cheese or feta.

6. Continue layering in this way until you have used up all the ingredients, finishing with a layer of sauce. Top with the reserved Parmesan, then bake for 25–30 minutes, until golden. Allow to cool before serving to your little one. This can be cut up or mashed with a fork for younger babies.

SIMPLE HADDOCK FISHCAKE BITES

PREP: 10–30 minutes

COOK: 40–50 minutes

MAKES: about 20 fishcakes, depending on size

200g (7oz) line-caught
  haddock
300ml (10fl oz/1¼ cups) milk
200g (7oz) potatoes, peeled
  and cut into chunks
100g (4oz) frozen peas
1 tsp chopped fresh mint
oil, for brushing

A great tasting fish recipe for your little one. Serve with some seasonal green vegetables like courgette, broccoli or some extra peas. For a different texture the fishcakes can be coated in polenta or breadcrumbs before baking.

1. Preheat the oven to 200°C/180°C fan/400°F/gas mark 6.

2. Place the haddock in a large pan, pour over the milk and poach over a low heat for about 5 minutes, or until the fish is cooked.

3. Cook the potatoes in a pan of boiling water for 12–15 minutes until soft, then drain. Cook the peas in a separate pan of boiling water for 3–4 minutes until cooked.

4. Carefully remove the skin and any bones from the fish and flake in with the potatoes. Add the drained peas and chopped mint and stir thoroughly.

5. Shape the mixture into fishcakes, in whatever shape or size you think your little one would prefer – you can get creative and make fish shapes if you like!

6. Brush each fishcake with a little oil then place on a baking tray. Bake for about 20 minutes, until golden. Allow to cool before serving.

PREP: under 10 minutes

COOK: 15–25 minutes

MAKES: 4–6 servings

120g long grain rice
1 tbsp olive oil
½ onion, thinly sliced
1 carrot, peeled and cut into
    5mm (¼in) dice
½ red (bell) pepper, cut into
    5mm (¼in) dice
½ tsp chinese five-spice
½ tsp ground ginger
250g skinless salmon fillets
2 handfuls of frozen peas
2 handfuls of beansprouts
juice of ½ lemon (optional)

A tasty Chinese-inspired dish that is a great way to introduce different spices and tastes to your little one.

1. Cook the rice until tender, following the instructions on the packet.

2. Heat the oil in a lidded frying pan (skillet) or wok over a medium heat and add the sliced onion. Fry, stirring, until cooked.

3. Add the carrot and red pepper to the pan with the five-spice and ground ginger. Place a lid on the wok or pan and cook the vegetables until the carrot is soft.

4. Add the whole salmon fillets to the pan and replace the lid. Cook for 5 minutes over a medium heat, then turn the salmon over and add the peas and beansprouts. Cook for a further 5 minutes.

5. Flake the salmon into manageable pieces. Stir in the cooked and drained rice, add the lemon juice, if using, and cook for a further 2 minutes before serving.

MOROCCAN CHICKPEAS & QUINOA

PREP: 10-30 minutes

COOK: 10-30 minutes

MAKES: 2 adult and 2 child portions

200g quinoa
100g dried apricots, finely chopped
1 tsp cumin seeds
1 tsp coriander seeds
olive oil, for frying
1 onion, finely chopped
1-2 garlic cloves, crushed
100g green beans, trimmed and cut into 1cm (½in) pieces
1 tsp mixed spice
400g (14oz) can chickpeas, drained and rinsed
2 large handfuls of spinach, leaves shredded
2 tbsp chopped parsley

A delicious vegan dish that is perfectly balanced and gently spiced. Asparagus makes a great seasonal alternative to the green beans if you prefer. You can also substitute the quinoa for rice or couscous if gluten isn't a problem. Serve warm or cold as a complete vegan meal or, if serving as an accompaniment to meat or fish, you can leave out the chickpeas if you wish. For younger babies you can cut the beans and apricots up very finely and then mash everything together at the end for a less chunky texture.

1. Cook the quinoa according to the packet instructions. Meanwhile, soak the chopped apricots in a bowl of hot water. Crush the cumin and coriander seeds in a pestle and mortar (or you can use ground spices if you prefer).

2. Heat a little olive oil in a pan, add the onion and garlic and sauté over a low heat until just soft. Add the green beans, crushed seeds and mixed spice and stir together. Add the chickpeas for another couple of minutes until coated and heated through, then add the spinach and cook for another minute until just wilted.

3. Drain the quinoa, stir through the spiced vegetables, then drain the apricots and stir in as well along with the chopped parsley.

4. Chop or mash to the right consistency before serving.

CURRIED COCONUT
CAULIFLOWER BAKE

PREP: 10-30 minutes

COOK: 30-45 minutes

MAKES: 4 adult and
1 baby portion

1 whole cauliflower, cut into
  bite-sized florets
150g (5oz) quinoa, rinsed in
  cold water

FOR THE CURRY SAUCE:
2 tbsp coconut oil (or use
  olive oil or butter)
2 tbsp coconut flour
  (or use plain wheat flour
  if not gluten-free)
400ml (14fl oz) can
  coconut milk
2 tsp curry powder
1 tsp garam masala

This slightly unusual dish can easily be made in advance and stored in the fridge for a couple of days, or it can be frozen. If you are reheating this dish, cover with foil or a lid and bake for about 20 minutes covered, then a further 10 minutes without the foil until the crumble is golden. Always ensure it is piping hot in the centre.

1. Preheat the oven to 200°C/180°C fan/400°F/gas mark 6.

2. Steam the cauliflower until just tender, about 15 minutes. Cook the quinoa at the same time in the boiling water underneath your steaming basket, as they take the same time to cook. If you don't have a steamer, simply boil the quinoa and cauliflower together in a large pan until cooked.

3. Meanwhile make your curry sauce. Put the coconut oil and flour into a pan and gently heat, stirring constantly, until a paste is formed – this is called a 'roux' and will thicken your sauce. As soon as the paste forms, start to add the coconut milk, gradually stirring it in bit by bit. Make sure you keep stirring continuously to avoid any lumps. Once all the milk is added the sauce should begin to thicken. (If it thickens too quickly, reduce the heat a little and keep stirring over a low heat until it is smooth, and custard-like in consistency.) Stir in the curry powder and garam masala.

4. Drain the cauliflower and quinoa and spread out evenly in a 30 x 25cm (12 x 10in) baking dish. Pour the sauce over the top and mix together carefully. At this point you can mash the cooked cauliflower a little more into the sauce if you prefer, which makes it easier for little ones to eat.

5. Finally make your crumble topping by crushing the cumin and coriander seeds until very fine in a pestle and mortar (or use ready-ground spices). Crush the cashews until fine – either with the pestle and mortar or in a food processor. Ensure the cashews are finely crushed, especially for younger babies. Mix the spices, cashews and desiccated coconut together, then sprinkle evenly over the top of your dish.

1 tsp cumin seeds
1 tsp coriander seeds
100g (4oz) cashews
(see note)
30g (1oz) desiccated
coconut

6. Bake for 10–15 minutes, until the crumble is golden on top and piping hot throughout. For younger babies you can mash the cauliflower up a little more with a fork.

NOTE: if your little one can't have nuts, you can replace the cashews with the same amount of oats, rubbed together with a knob of coconut oil, or olive oil. These oils replace the natural oil present in the cashews to create a golden crumble topping.

PREP: 60+ minutes

COOK: 30–40 minutes

MAKES: 2 adult and
1 baby portion

2 large handfuls of cooked
   turkey or chicken
drizzle of coconut oil or
   olive oil, for marinating
3 tsp mild curry powder
1 tsp garam masala
1 onion, finely chopped
2 garlic cloves, crushed
2cm (¾in) piece of fresh
   ginger, peeled and grated
½ x 400g (14oz) can
   chopped tomatoes for
   the red curry
½ x 400g (14oz) can coconut
   milk for the green curry
2 large handfuls of cooked
   vegetables of your choice,
   such as leeks, broccoli,
   parsnips, sprouts (cut
   into bite-sized chunks if
   feeding to little ones)
cooked basmati rice,
   to serve
fresh coriander (cilantro) and
   squeeze of lime, to finish
   (optional)

Serve this curry with rice and top with fresh coriander and a squeeze of lime. The curry can be mashed a little or blended to a purée for young babies. Additional spices and chilli powder can be added separately at the end for adults. For a vegetarian version swap the turkey or chicken for extra vegetables.

1. Tear or cut up the turkey or chicken into bite-sized pieces (smaller for younger babies). Add to a bowl with a drizzle of oil, the curry powder and garam masala. Rub all over the meat and leave to marinate, covered with cling film (plastic wrap), in the fridge for at least 1 hour – ideally overnight so the flavour really intensifies.

2. Add a drizzle of oil to a large, wide-based pan and add the onion. Sauté over a low–medium heat for 5 minutes, then add the garlic and ginger. Add the spiced meat and sauté gently for a minute or two so the spices begin to smell delicious.

3. To make both the red and green curry, divide the mixture into 2 separate heavy-based pans at this point. To one pan, add one handful of the cooked vegetables and the chopped tomatoes and stir well – this is your red curry. Add the remaining vegetables and the coconut milk to the other pan to make your green curry; stir well.

4. Cook both curries for about 20 minutes, long enough for the flavours to infuse and the meat to heat thoroughly, without the vegetables going mushy. Add a little extra liquid (either canned tomatoes or coconut milk) if either curry looks a little dry. (For a simpler version, don't halve the mixture and choose to make just one curry, doubling the quantity of either canned chopped tomatoes or coconut milk.

5. Serve the curries with freshly cooked basmati rice and finish with a sprinkling of coriander and a squeeze of lime juice, if liked.

....

TOP TIP: to peel fresh ginger, simply scrape it with the side of a teaspoon – the skin comes off easily.

AUBERGINE & CHICKPEA TAGINE

12+
months

PREP: 10–30 minutes

COOK: 40–50 minutes

MAKES: 2 adult and
2 child portions

FOR THE TAGINE:
2 tbsp olive oil
1 red onion, thinly sliced
3 garlic cloves, crushed
1 tbsp freshly grated ginger
1 tsp ground cinnamon
2 tsp ground cumin
2 tsp ground coriander
1 tsp ground turmeric
1 tsp smoked paprika
300g (10oz) aubergine
(eggplant), cut into 2cm
(¾in) dice
175g (6oz) red (bell) pepper,
cut into 2cm (¾in) dice
2 tbsp tomato paste
400g (14oz) can chopped
tomatoes
175g (6oz) dried apricots,
roughly chopped
500–750ml (16–25fl
oz/2-3 cups) homemade
vegetable stock or water

CONTINUED OVERLEAF →

This tasty vegetarian main can be enjoyed by the all family and is a great way of introducing different tastes and textures to your little one. For younger babies a portion can be blended roughly to a mash consistency or a smooth purée. Toddlers and older children can enjoy everything although for younger toddlers you may want to cut up the veggies and mash the chickpeas and mix with the couscous, leaving the salad for the bigger ones.

1. Heat olive oil in a large pan or casserole over a low–medium heat. Add the onion and the garlic and fry gently until soft, about 5–10 minutes.

2. Add the ginger and ground spices and fry for 1 minute, then add the diced aubergine and red pepper. Fry for 5 minutes, stirring regularly.

3. Add the tomato paste, chopped tomatoes, apricots and 500ml (16fl oz/ 2 cups) water or stock. Cook, half-covered, over a medium heat for about 20 minutes, until the vegetables are cooked. Top up with more stock or water if needed.

4. Add the drained chickpeas and black olives and cook, uncovered, for another 5 minutes. Season to taste with lemon juice and black pepper.

5. Meanwhile, make the salad. Put the grated beetroot into a bowl with the raisins and chopped herbs. In a separate bowl mix together the olive oil, cinnamon, cumin, lemon juice and garlic to make a dressing. Pour over the grated beetroot, toss to combine and set aside. →

AUBERGINE & CHICKPEA TAGINE CONTINUED

400g (14oz) can chickpeas, drained and rinsed
150g (5oz) pitted black olives
3 tbsp lemon juice
freshly ground black pepper

FOR THE BEETROOT (BEET) AND HERB SALAD:
150g (5oz) raw beetroot (beets), peeled and grated
50g (2oz) raisins
2 tbsp chopped fresh mint leaves
2 tbsp chopped fresh coriander (cilantro) leaves
3 tbsp olive oil
½ tsp ground cinnamon
½ tsp ground cumin
2½ tbsp lemon juice
1 garlic clove, crushed

FOR THE TURMERIC COUSCOUS:
200g (7oz) couscous
¾ tsp ground turmeric
2 tbsp chopped coriander (cilantro) leaves

6. Make the couscous just before you're ready to serve. Mix the couscous and turmeric together in a heatproof bowl. Add enough boiling water to fully cover the couscous. Cover the bowl with cling film (plastic wrap) or a tea towel and leave to rest for about 5 minutes. Fluff with a fork, cover again and leave to rest for a further 2 minutes. Add the chopped coriander and toss well.

7. Serve up the tagine with the couscous and the beetroot salad on the side.

LEMONY CHICKEN GOUJONS

PREP: 10–30 minutes

COOK: 25–30 minutes

MAKES: 2 adult and 2 toddler portions

oil, for greasing
3 slices of wholemeal bread
(slightly stale bread is
perfect)
pinch of freshly ground
black pepper
grated zest of 1 lemon
2 eggs
4 heaped tbsp plain flour
4 chicken breasts

A no-junk favourite for all the family. These go brilliantly with a zesty lemon dip – simply mix a squeeze of lemon juice and a pinch of lemon zest into some Greek yoghurt. To make this more of a main meal serve with some seasonal vegetables.

1. Preheat the oven to 200°C/180°C fan/400°F/gas mark 6 and lightly grease a baking tray.

2. Whizz the bread into breadcrumbs in a food processor then tip on to a plate and add some black pepper and the lemon zest. (If you don't have a food processor you can create breadcrumbs by rubbing each slice through a fine sieve.) Beat the eggs together in a shallow bowl and put the flour on to a separate plate.

3. Cut the chicken breasts into strips (goujons) and then dip each one first in the flour, then into the beaten egg, then into the breadcrumbs, pressing them lightly to coat.

4. Place the goujons on the baking tray and bake for 25–30 minutes, until golden and cooked through. Turn over halfway through cooking.

MOREISH SAVOURY CRUMBLE

PREP: 10–30 minutes

COOK: 40–50 minutes

MAKES: 6 small or 4 large portions

FOR THE FILLING:
400ml (14fl oz/1 ⅔ cups) hot vegetable stock (ideally homemade with no added salt, or a low salt alternative)
1 parsnip, peeled and diced
4 small (or 2 large) carrots, peeled and diced
300g butternut squash, peeled and diced
1 large (or 2 small) leek, finely chopped
small bunch of thyme, leaves chopped
50g (2oz) Parmesan cheese or vegetarian equivalent, grated
250ml (8fl oz/1 cup) single (light) cream
100g (4oz) feta cheese, crumbled

FOR THE CRUMBLE:
100g (4oz) unsalted butter, diced →

200g (7oz/1½ cups) wholemeal flour (gluten free if required)
50g (2oz/¼ cup) oats (gluten free if required)
50g (2oz) Parmesan cheese or vegetarian equivalent, grated
sunflower, pumpkin or sesame seeds (optional)

This is a super-simple and delicious winter warmer. It has that moreish quality of a sweet crumble, but with seasonal savoury ingredients. All your family will enjoy tucking into this creamy dish. Serve warm with some fresh greens or salad, or you could serve as a side dish with some fish or meat. Mash or blend down for younger babies.

1. Preheat the oven to 200°C/180°C fan/400°F/gas mark 6.

2. Bring the stock to the boil in a large pan, then add the chopped parsnip, carrot and butternut squash. Reduce the heat to a rapid simmer and cook for about 10 minutes until tender. Add the leek, cover with a lid and simmer for a further 5 minutes, then remove from the heat.

3. Meanwhile make the crumble topping. Rub the butter into the flour with your fingertips until you get a breadcrumb-like texture. Mix in the oats and Parmesan, then set aside.

4. Drain the cooked vegetables, discarding any remaining stock and tip them into an ovenproof dish. Scatter over the thyme and Parmesan, then stir into the vegetables with the cream. Scatter the feta evenly over the dish and finally top with the crumble, adding the seeds, if using (you can finely chop the seeds if you like, especially if for younger babies).

5. Bake for 20–25 minutes, until the crumble is golden; allow to cool before serving.

NOTE: You can make this in advance and reheat the whole dish. If reheating bake for at least 30 minutes, or until it is piping hot in the centre. If cooking for longer, prevent the crumble from burning by covering with foil. The crumble topping takes about 20 minutes to cook.

PORK & APPLE BURGERS

  (gf) (df) ❄

PREP: 10–30 minutes

COOK: 10–15 minutes

MAKES: 4–6 burgers

250g minced pork
½ medium Bramley apple,
   peeled, cored and finely
   diced
½ onion, finely diced
sprinkle of thyme and
   oregano (fresh or dried)
sprinkle of freshly ground
   black pepper
1 garlic clove, finely
   chopped
olive oil, for frying

A great tasting burger for toddlers to enjoy. Delicious served in a mini bread roll. You can make these in advance and keep in the fridge, covered, for 1–2 days – they also freeze layered between sheets of baking parchment. Defrost thoroughly in the fridge before cooking.

1. Put all the ingredients, except the oil, in a bowl and mix together – it's best to do this with your hands as this will ensure the small ingredients get mixed into the pork.

2. Divide the mixture evenly into 4 or 6 portions, depending on how many burgers you want to make. Roll each in your hand and flatten into small mini burgers.

3. To cook the burgers, heat some olive oil in a frying pan (skillet), add the burgers and fry over a medium heat for 5 minutes on each side. Make sure the burger is cooked through (not pink in the middle) but take care not to burn them!

Snacks
& Treats

ROASTED PEAR & RHUBARB WITH VANILLA

   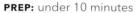

PREP: under 10 minutes

COOK: 25-30 minutes

MAKES: 3-6 servings

2 pears, cored, peeled and
   quartered
1 small pink rhubarb stem,
   cut into 2cm (¾in) pieces
a few drops of vanilla extract
2 tbsp water

An irresistible recipe that makes the most of delicious rhubarb – great for weaning. Can be served with yoghurt, or a dairy-free alternative, for a creamier taste for little ones aged 6 months or older.

1. Preheat the oven to 180°C/160°C fan/350°F/gas mark 4.

2. Place the pear and the rhubarb pieces in a small roasting tin and mix with the vanilla extract. Pour the water into the bottom of the tin and then place the tin in the oven and roast for 25-30 minutes until the fruit is tender.

3. Allow the fruit to cool before blending until smooth with a hand blender. You can add a little more water to get the right consistency for your little one.

CARROT HUMMOUS

6+
months

PREP: 10-20 minutes

COOK: 20-25 minutes

MAKES: 1 pot

250g (9oz) carrots, scrubbed
1 garlic clove
½ tbsp olive oil
½ x 400g (14oz) can
   chickpeas, drained and
   rinsed
½ tsp ground cumin
1 ½ tbsp orange juice

This homemade hummous with delicious carrots and a hint of spice is quick and simple to make. Serve in sandwiches, spread on bread or as a delicious dip with steamed or raw veggie sticks.

1. Preheat the oven to 200°C/180°C fan/400°F/gas mark 6.

2. Top and tail the carrots, then cut into short sticks, leaving the skins on. Put into a small roasting tray with the garlic clove (still in its papery skin) and the olive oil. Shake the tray to completely coat the carrots and garlic in the oil. Pop into the oven to roast for 20-25 minutes until the carrots are golden and cooked through. Remove from the oven and leave to cool.

3. Tip the drained chickpeas into a blender. Squeeze the roasted garlic out of its skin and into the blender and add the roasted carrots, ground cumin and orange juice. Blend all the ingredients together until you have a hummous consistency.

4. Tip into a bowl, cover and store in the fridge for up to 3 days.

BEETROOT HUMMOUS

6+
months

PREP: under 10 minutes

MAKES: 1 pot

200g (7oz) cooked beetroot
   (beets), roughly chopped
½ x 400g (14oz) can
   chickpeas, drained and
   rinsed
1 small garlic clove, peeled
   (optional)
½ tsp ground cumin
1 tbsp olive oil
½ tbsp lemon juice

Colourful and tasty homemade hummous made with beetroot.

1. Simply add everything to a food processor or high-speed blender and blitz until smooth. Add a little water if needed to thin the mixture to your desired consistency.

2. Transfer to an airtight container and store in the fridge for up to 3 days.

RICE PUDDING

 7+ months

PREP: under 10 minutes

COOK: 30–35 minutes

MAKES: about 6 baby portions

50g (2oz) pudding rice
600ml (20fl oz/2½ cups)
**   full-fat milk**
a few drops of vanilla extract

A simple, warming classic, perfect for little ones as an after-dinner treat.

1. Put the rice and milk into a pan and place over a medium–high heat.

2. Bring to the boil, then reduce the heat, cover with a lid and simmer for 30–35 minutes, stirring occasionally.

3. Stir in the vanilla extract and allow to cool a little before serving.

RASPBERRY & YOGHURT LOLLIES

7+ months

PREP: under 10 minutes

FREEZE: overnight

MAKES: 6 servings

100g (4oz) raspberries
100g (4oz) natural yoghurt

A tasty treat for little ones.

1. Put the raspberries into a blender and blitz until smooth. We like the bits, but you could push the mixture through a sieve to get the seeds out and make it smoother, if you like.

2. Combine the raspberry purée with the yoghurt and then pour the mixture into six ice-lolly moulds. Put them in the freezer overnight, or until frozen.

3. To release the lollies from their moulds, dip them in hot water for a few seconds.

APPLE & CINNAMON MUFFINS

PREP: 10-20 minutes

COOK: 20-30 minutes

MAKES: 6 large or
12 small muffins

3 eggs
3 tbsp maple syrup
2 tsp ground cinnamon
120ml (4fl oz/½ cup) olive
oil (or use melted
coconut oil)
2 apples, grated
150g (5oz/generous 1 cup)
self-raising flour (use
gluten free if you prefer)

These muffins are naturally sweetened by the apple, maple syrup and cinnamon. You can even get older children involved in making these, helping to grate the apple, weigh flour and stir the ingredients together. Add chopped nuts or seeds for older children or dried fruit for added sweetness and texture.

1. Preheat the oven to 200°C/180°C fan/400°F/gas mark 6 and lightly grease a muffin tin (pan) with oil or line with paper muffin cases.

2. Beat the eggs in a large bowl with the maple syrup, cinnamon and olive oil (or gently melted coconut oil). Stir the apples into the egg mixture. Finally fold in the self-raising flour with a metal spoon.

3. Spoon evenly into the muffin holes or paper cases and bake for about 20 minutes, or until golden and cooked in the centre – stick a knife in the centre of a muffin to check they are cooked – it should come out clean. Transfer to a wire rack to cool.

VARIATIONS: Baking is a little trickier when it comes to experimenting as the consistency of ingredients makes quite a difference to the end result. However, you could try varying the fruit and spice in these little muffins along with the season and see what result you get. The base recipe is fairly reliable so most fruits should work. Try pear and ginger or banana, walnut and fig, or perhaps raspberry and orange zest? If the fruit is a lot wetter than the original grated apple (like mashed banana might be), you can reduce the oil by a tiny amount or increase the flour a little.

BLACKBERRY DROPS

PREP: 20–30 minutes

COOK: 35–45 minutes

MAKES: 25–30 drops

2 pears, peeled, cored and
   quartered
a little water (if required)
150g (5oz) unsalted butter
   (or use coconut oil)
4 eggs
6 tbsp maple syrup
½ tsp vanilla extract
100g (4oz/1 cup) ground
   almonds (see page 7)
150g (5oz/generous 1 cup)
   self-raising flour (use
   gluten free if you prefer)
25–30 blackberries

VARIATIONS: Vary the fruit
along with the season –
raspberries and blueberries
work well, or you can chop
larger fruit into chunks,
such as apricots, banana or
mango. The pear purée can
be replaced with mashed
banana or another fruit purée
of your choice.

These tasty little drops are easy and quick to make, and older children will enjoy getting involved. These make a delicious teatime treat, tasty pudding or afternoon snack. Keep for up to 3 days in an airtight container in a cool place or in the fridge.

1. Start by making a purée with the pears. Steam until soft, about 20 minutes, either using a steamer or by placing in a colander over a pan of simmering water and covering (you could boil the pears instead, if you prefer, but steaming retains more of the nutrients).

2. In a bowl, blend the pears to a smooth purée, adding some water if required – just enough to get a smooth consistency. A hand blender will give the smoothest texture, but a food processor or blender can also be used.

3. Stir the butter or coconut oil into the warm purée to gently melt it, or if the purée is cold, gently warm together in a pan over a low heat until just melted. Then allow to cool. If you are using a pre-made purée from the freezer you will need 250ml (9floz) purée. Allow to defrost overnight, then gently warm through with the butter or oil.

4. Preheat the oven to 160°C/140°C fan/325°F/gas 3 and line 2 large baking trays with baking parchment.

5. Whisk the eggs, maple syrup, vanilla and cooled purée together in a large bowl. Stir in the ground almonds then sift in the flour and lightly stir using a metal spoon. Don't over-mix to avoid knocking out too much air.

6. Use a tablespoon to drop small round blobs of the mixture on to your lined baking trays, leaving at least 2cm (¾in) between them. Press a blackberry into the centre of each drop (children love to help with this).

7. Bake for 15 minutes, or until golden and risen. Eat warm or allow to cool on a wire rack.

BLUEBERRY & FIG FLAPJACKS

PREP: under 10 minutes

COOK: 20-30 minutes

MAKES: about 15 flapjacks

200g (7oz/1 cup) oats
  (gluten free if required)
100g (4oz/1 cup) ground
  almonds (see page 7)
100g (4oz) fresh blueberries
4 dried figs, chopped into
  small bite-sized pieces
100g (4oz) unsalted butter
4 tbsp maple syrup

These delicious little flapjacks can be made with whatever fruit is in season, but blueberries are particularly good. These make the perfect snack or dessert for your little one or could be served as part of a healthy breakfast on the go, with some extra fruit and a glass of milk. As these contain very little sugar to preserve them, and they have fresh fruit in, they only keep for about 3 days. They will stay fresher in the fridge or somewhere cool.

1. Preheat the oven to 200°C/180°C fan/400°F/gas mark 6 and line a 30 x 15cm (12 x 6in) baking tin with baking parchment.

2. In a large bowl, mix the oats and ground almonds. Throw in the blueberries and chopped dried figs and stir together.

3. Gently melt the butter in a small pan over a low heat with the maple syrup. Pour this over the oat mixture and stir to coat.

4. Tip the mixture into the prepared tin and press down firmly. Bake for about 20 minutes until golden. Allow to cool slightly in the tin, then cut up into about 15 square flapjacks – delicious!

CRANBERRY & ORANGE CHRISTMAS BISCUITS

PREP: 20–40 minutes

COOK: 35–45 minutes

MAKES: about 25 biscuits, depending on your cutter

FOR THE BISCUITS:
200g (7oz/1½ cups) plain flour (see note below)
½ tsp baking powder
60g (2½oz) cold unsalted butter (you could also use coconut butter), diced
grated zest of 1 orange
50g (2oz) dried cranberries, roughly chopped
60ml (2fl oz/¼ cup) orange juice

OPTIONAL DECORATIONS:
desiccated coconut
coconut oil or maple syrup

NOTE: You can replace half the flour with ground almonds if you prefer – this gives the biscuits a really lovely soft texture.

These tasty little Christmas treats are a fun activity to do with your little ones and make the perfect Christmas gift too. Keep in an airtight container for up to 4 or 5 days.

1. Preheat the oven to 180°C/160°C fan/350°F/gas mark 5 and line a baking sheet or two with baking parchment.

2. Sift the flour and baking powder into a large bowl, then rub in the butter with your fingertips until it resembles breadcrumbs (or pulse together in a food processor).

3. Add the orange zest and cranberries and combine thoroughly (chopping the cranberries will give a better distribution through the biscuits). Add the orange juice a little at a time and mix to create a dough that is smooth but not sticky. Add a little extra juice or flour to get the right consistency.

4. Roll out the dough on a lightly floured surface, then cut out Christmas shapes with the cutters of your choice. Use a straw to make holes, so that the biscuits can be hung from your Christmas tree.

5. Use a palette knife to carefully lift the biscuit shapes off the work surface and on to your lined baking sheets. Re-roll the leftover dough and cut out more shapes. This is where you can let your little ones choose their favourite Christmas shapes and have a go at cutting their own biscuits.

6. Bake for 10–15 minutes, or until just golden – keep a watchful eye as they can burn very quickly. Transfer to a wire rack and wait if you can before nibbling!

7. Add a little Christmas decoration to the top of the biscuits, if you like: simply spread the top of each biscuit with a little maple syrup or coconut oil, then press sticky-side down into a pile of desiccated coconut, for a fantastic 'snowy' topping. These biscuits will taste more delicious to your little ones, knowing that they helped make them!

BANANA & BLACKBERRY YOGHURT ICE CREAM

PREP: 10–20 minutes

FREEZE: 3 hours, plus overnight

MAKES: 4-8 portions

½ **medium banana**
100g (4oz) blackberries
80g (3oz) raisins
200g (7oz) Greek yoghurt
1 tsp vanilla extract

A healthy snack that is great for hot summer days but tasty at any time of the year. Why not serve with some halved blackberries and banana slices?

1. Mash the banana with a fork in a bowl. In a separate bowl blitz the blackberries, raisins and 2 tablespoons of the yoghurt with a hand blender. Stir through the mashed banana and then push it all through a sieve to make it really smooth.

2. Add the remaining yoghurt and vanilla extract to the fruit and mix together then pour into a freezer-safe container (plastic or Tupperware is good). Make sure you only fill up to halfway.

3. Freeze for 2 hours, or until it becomes firm around the edges. Use a fork to stir up the mixture and break down any ice crystals. Re-freeze for another hour and repeat the stirring process with a fork if necessary. Freeze overnight and enjoy the next day.

PEANUT BUTTER COOKIES

PREP: under 10 minutes

COOK: 12–15 minutes

MAKES: 12 cookies

1 ripe banana (overripe
   is fine)
50g (2oz) crunchy 100%
   peanut butter (with no
   added sugar or salt)
1 tbsp milk
1 tbsp maple syrup
¼ tsp vanilla extract
100g (4oz/½ cup) rolled oats
20g (¾oz) plain flour
2 tbsp raisins

These tasty cookies, with their slightly cake-like texture, can be made with our very own raisins.

1. Preheat the oven to 180°C/160°C fan/350°F/gas mark 4.

2. In a large bowl, mash the banana with a fork until smooth. Add the peanut butter, milk, maple syrup and vanilla and mix well.

3. Add the oats, flour and raisins and stir until combined.

4. Place 12 evenly sized spoonfuls of the mixture on to an ungreased baking tray, spacing them well apart, then press down on each one to squash slightly.

5. Bake for 12–15 minutes, then leave to cool on the baking tray. The cookies should be crunchy on the outside with a slightly soft middle.

CRISPY GREEN BEANS WITH A MAPLE DIP

12+ months

PREP: 10–30 minutes

COOK: 15–20 minutes

MAKES: 2 servings

75g (3oz) breadcrumbs
(gluten free, if required)
1 tsp garlic powder
4 tbsp Parmesan cheese
or vegetarian equivalent
pinch of freshly ground
black pepper
1 egg
150g (5oz) green beans
(not too thin), trimmed
spray or drizzle of olive oil

FOR THE MAPLE
MUSTARD DIP:
100g (4oz) crème fraîche
2–3 tsp Dijon mustard
1 tbsp maple syrup (or
honey for children over
12 months)
½ tbsp lemon juice
2 tsp dried tarragon
1 small garlic clove, crushed

These crispy green beans make a quick and healthy snack and a great alternative to chips. Serve with our maple mustard dip for a little twist. For little ones over 12 months you can replace the maple syrup in the dip with honey if you prefer. Make sure you cut the beans in half or smaller bite-sized pieces for little ones.

1. Preheat the oven to 200°C/180°C fan/400°F/gas mark 6 and line a baking tray with baking parchment.

2. Make the dip by mixing all the ingredients together until well combined. Cover and put in the fridge until needed.

3. On a shallow plate, mix together the breadcrumbs, garlic powder, Parmesan and black pepper. Beat the egg in a shallow bowl. Dip each green bean in the egg mixture then coat all over by dipping them in the breadcrumbs mixture.

4. Place the coated green beans on the lined baking tray and spray or drizzle with some olive oil. Bake for 15–20 minutes, until golden and crispy. Serve straight away with the dip on the side.

TOMATO & SWEETCORN SALSA

PREP: under 10 minutes

MAKES: 1 bowl, enough for 2 adults and 2 children

150g (5oz) cherry tomatoes
small handful of fresh coriander (cilantro)
small handful of fresh parsley
¼ red onion
3 tbsp cooked sweetcorn
1 small garlic clove
2 tsp lemon juice

This fresh, tasty salsa is delicious as a dip for raw or steamed vegetables. Adults could also add a little chopped fresh chilli to their portion if they fancy a spicy alternative. You could also try roasting the tomatoes first for a slightly different flavour if you like.

1. In a blender or food processor, blitz all the ingredients together very lightly on a pulse setting until you get a rough textured salsa. Be careful not to over-blend as the tomatoes can release quite a lot of water. If this does happen, simply drain off some of the excess liquid before serving. For a smoother texture you could also try blending the other ingredients first then adding the tomatoes at the end.

2. Alternatively, make a slightly chunkier salsa by very finely chopping all the ingredients by hand and mixing together.

PARSNIP CHIPS

12+ months

PREP: under 10 minutes

COOK: 30-40 minutes

MAKES: 2-4 servings

3 large parsnips, peeled and
   sliced into chip shapes
2 tsp olive oil
freshly ground black pepper

A simple way to make great tasting chips that the whole family can enjoy! Serve these with a variety of different dishes such as chicken goujons or homemade fish fingers. Why not experiment by adding some herbs or spices?

1. Preheat the oven to 200°C/180°C fan/400°F/gas mark 6.

2. Put the parsnips into a bowl, drizzle with the olive oil and grind over some black pepper. Mix thoroughly with your hands to make sure all the parsnips chips are coated.

3. Tip onto a baking tray and spread out in an even layer. Bake in the oven for 30-40 minutes until the parsnips are soft in the middle and golden on the outside.

INDEX

ACKNOWLEDGEMENTS

We've got lots and lots of lovely people to thank who have helped bring this book to life.

Firstly, a big thank you to all the Organix team. Without their dedication, hard work and commitment to making things better, this book would not have been a possibility.

Thanks to our good friends Annabelle Randles and Kirsty Bethell, as well as their families, who experimented and taste-tested all our recipes to make sure they were scrummy enough for you!

To the little superstars, Avaya, Kaif, Phoenix, Evie, Theo and Piper, who appear in our book and the great team who photographed them; Liz and Max Hamilton, as well as food stylist Kitty Coles, prop stylist Faye Wears and designer Louise Evans; you have made this book really shine.

The lovely team at Penguin Random House, thanks for believing in us and what we stand for.

But the biggest thank you goes to all the little learners (and bigger ones!) who love Organix, without you, we wouldn't be able to do this.